2. Remember your responsibility

Peter began his first letter with a joyous paean of praise to lift his readers' spirits and help them focus on God rather than on their circumstances: "Blessed be the God and Father of our Lord Jesus Christ, who according to His great mercy has caused us to be born again to a living hope through the resurrection of Jesus Christ from the dead, to obtain an inheritance which is imperishable and undefiled and will not fade away, reserved in heaven for you, who are protected by the power of God through faith for a salvation ready to be revealed in the last time" (vv. 3-5).

Although the verb "be" in verse 3 ("Blessed be the God . . . ") is the main verb, it is implied in the Greek text rather than stated. The text could be literally translated, "Bless the God and Father of our Lord Jesus Christ." In short, "Bless God." It is both a doxology and a command. While directing our hearts upward in the joy of adoration and the anticipation of our future inheritance, Peter reminds us to bless God when difficult circumstances arise.

3. Remember your inheritance

One key to experiencing joy amid trials is to understand God's provisions for us. Although we are aliens in this world (1 Pet. 1:1) and treated as outcasts, we are citizens of heaven and recipients of all that God has promised us in Christ. We must therefore learn to look beyond our earthly troubles to our eternal inheritance. That will motivate us to praise God.

a) Our inheritance affirmed

(1) By the Lord Jesus

Jesus said, "The King will say to those on His right, 'Come, you who are blessed of My Father, inherit the kingdom prepared for you from the foundation of the world'" (Matt. 25:34). That kingdom is part of our inheritance.

9

(2) By the apostle Paul

    (*a*) Acts 26:18—Paul was commissioned by Christ to preach to the Gentiles "so that they may turn from darkness to light and from the dominion of Satan to God, in order that they may receive forgiveness of sins and an inheritance among those who have been sanctified by faith in [Christ]."

    (*b*) Ephesians 1:10-18—We learn that the source of our inheritance is Jesus Christ, the pledge of our inheritance is the Holy Spirit, and the understanding of our inheritance comes through spiritual enlightenment.

    (*c*) Colossians 1:12—"[Give] thanks to the Father, who has qualified us to share in the inheritance of the saints in light."

(3) By the writer of Hebrews

Hebrews 9:15 says, "[Christ] is the mediator of a new covenant, in order that . . . those who have been called may receive the promise of the eternal inheritance."

b) Our inheritance defined

(1) Its lexical definition

The Greek word translated "inheritance" in 1 Peter 1:4 (*klēronomia*) describes possessions passed down from generation to generation—a legacy one received because he was a family member. It's not something you earn or purchase.

In addition to the promise of a future inheritance, *klēronomia* also includes the idea of an inheritance that one presently possesses and enjoys (Fritz Rienecker and Cleon Rogers, *Linguistic Key to the Greek New Testament* [Grand Rapids: Zondervan, 1982], p. 744).

Our Great Salvation

Our Great Salvation

by
John MacArthur, Jr.

"GRACE TO YOU"
P.O. Box 4000
Panorama City, CA   91412

ISBN: 0-8024-5340-6

1 2 3 4 5 6 Printing/LC/Year 94 93 92 91 90

Printed in the United States of America

Contents

1. Adoring God for Our Eternal Inheritance—Part 1   7
   Tape GC 60-5—1 Peter 1:3

2. Adoring God for Our Eternal Inheritance—Part 2   23
   Tape GC 60-6—1 Peter 1:3-5

3. The Joy of Salvation—Part 1   41
   Tape GC 60-7—1 Peter 1:6-7*a*

4. The Joy of Salvation—Part 2   55
   Tape GC 60-8—1 Peter 1:7*b*-9

5. The Greatness of Our Salvation   71
   Tape GC 60-9—1 Peter 1:10-12

Scripture Index   89

Topical Index   93

These Bible studies are taken from messages delivered by Pastor-Teacher John MacArthur, Jr., at Grace Community Church in Panorama City, California. These messages have been combined into a 5-tape album titled *Our Great Salvation*. You may purchase this series either in an attractive vinyl cassette album or as individual cassettes. To purchase these tapes, request the album *Our Great Salvation*, or ask for the tapes by their individual GC numbers. Please consult the current price list; then, send your order, making your check payable to:

The Master's Communication
P.O. Box 4000
Panorama City, CA 91412

Or call the following toll-free number:
1-800-55-GRACE

1
Adoring God
for Our Eternal Inheritance—Part 1

Outline

Introduction
A. Peter's Readers
B. Peter's Reminders
  1. Remember your identity
  2. Remember your responsibility
  3. Remember your inheritance
    a) Our inheritance affirmed
      (1) By the Lord Jesus
      (2) By the apostle Paul
      (3) By the writer of Hebrews
    b) Our inheritance defined
      (1) Its lexical definition
      (2) Its Jewish origin
      (3) Its spiritual manifestation
    c) Our inheritance illustrated
      (1) The problem
      (2) The picture
      (3) The application
    d) Our inheritance described
      (1) We inherit salvation
      (2) We inherit God
      (3) We inherit Christ
      (4) We inherit the Holy Spirit

Lesson

I. The Source of Our Inheritance (v. 3*a*)
   A. Our Blessed God
   B. Our Father God
      1. A new identity for God
      2. An affirmation of Christ's divinity
         a) By Christ Himself
         b) By Paul
         c) By John
   C. Our Redeemer God
   D. Our Personal God

Conclusion

Introduction

Every believer experiences times of difficulty, hostility, persecution, and rejection. First Peter 1:3-5 teaches us that adoring God is a key factor in maintaining a proper perspective during such times.

   A. Peter's Readers

   Although they were scattered throughout northern Asia Minor—a fair distance from Rome—they faced mounting persecution that resulted from the burning of Rome, for which Emperor Nero had blamed the Christians.

   B. Peter's Reminders

   1. Remember your identity

   Peter said that all believers should expect persecution because we are "a chosen race, a royal priesthood, a holy nation, a people for God's own possession" (1 Pet. 2:9). As such we are at odds with an evil world and will incur its hostility. Instead of being intimidated by threats of persecution, we should follow the example of Christ, who entrusted His life to the Father (1 Pet. 2:21-23).

(2) Its Jewish origin

Klēronomia would remind Peter's Jewish readers of their forefathers' Old Testament inheritance. The Septuagint (the Greek translation of the Old Testament) uses the word to describe the portion of the Promised Land that was appointed to every Jewish tribe and family as an earthly inheritance (Deut. 15:4; 19:10).

That inheritance was first promised to Abraham (Gen. 17:8), but his descendants had to experience the bondage of Egypt and the chastening of the wilderness wanderings before they could enter the Promised Land.

(3) Its spiritual manifestation

As Israel received Canaan as an earthly inheritance, so Christians have a spiritual inheritance that is "reserved in heaven" (1 Pet. 1:4).

c) Our inheritance illustrated

(1) The problem

In the New Testament, Christians are called the children of God (Rom. 8:16). That name is appropriate not only because God is our Father but also because we, like children, lack a mature understanding of our inheritance. Although we are "heirs of God and fellow heirs with Christ" (Rom. 8:17), the fullness of our inheritance has not yet been made known to us (1 John 3:2).

(2) The picture

Our lack of understanding is analogous to a child prince who in his immaturity cannot grasp the significance of the riches and honor he will inherit as the king's son. Consequently he doesn't think or act like a king. He may even throw childish temper tantrums over meaningless displeasures that pale

11

in comparison to the overwhelming inheritance he will one day receive.

Throughout his youth he is strictly disciplined by his parents because they want him to mature into a man whose behavior befits a king. As the years go by, he slowly begins to understand the value of his inheritance.

(3) The application

We are like that little prince. We don't fully understand "all that God has prepared for those who love him" (1 Cor. 2:9). Like children, we often react inappropriately when circumstances are unfavorable or we don't get what we want. Sometimes the Lord has to discipline us to correct our behavior.

Peter helps us to respond properly by reminding us of the nature of our inheritance. Paul used a similar approach with the Colossian believers: "Set your mind on the things above, not on the things that are on earth" (Col. 3:2). Similarly, Jesus said that if we make the Father's kingdom and righteousness our first priorities, the necessities of life will be supplied to us (Matt. 6:33). John said, "Do not love the world, nor the things in the world" (1 John 2:15).

We must take our eyes off the world and focus on God, adoring Him for our eternal inheritance.

d) Our inheritance described

Our inheritance is multi-faceted.

(1) We inherit salvation

One aspect of our inheritance is "a salvation ready to be revealed in the last time" (1 Pet. 1:5). That refers to the fullness of our salvation. We can look beyond our present troubles and bless God for our eternal salvation.

12

(*a*) The nature of our salvation

The Greek word translated "salvation" speaks of a rescue or deliverance. In verse 5 it refers to our full and final deliverance from the curse of the law; the power and presence of sin; and from grief, pain, death, and judgment.

The Three Tenses of Salvation

1. Past tense

Some passages of Scripture refer to salvation in the past tense: we *have been* saved. For example, Peter said, "God . . . has caused us to be born again" (1 Pet. 1:3), and, "You have been born again" (1 Pet. 1:23). We were saved when we believed in Christ.

2. Present tense

Other passages of Scripture refer to salvation in the present tense: we *are being* saved. We have received eternal life, but the Lord keeps on cleansing us as we live in this world of sin (1 John 1:9).

Ephesians 2:8 says, "By grace you have been saved." The Greek text literally says, "By grace you are having been saved." That indicates a past action with continuing results (Kenneth Wuest, *Word Studies in the Greek New Testament: Ephesians and Colossians* [Grand Rapids: Eerdmans, 1953], p. 66).

3. Future tense

Other portions of Scripture refer to salvation in the future tense: we *shall be* saved. We will be fully and forever delivered from sin and judgment in the future. That's our ultimate eternal inheritance.

In 1 Thessalonians 1:9-10 Paul thanked God for the Thessalonian believers, who turned to God from idols and were waiting for the return of Jesus to deliver them from the wrath to come. Romans 13:11 says, "Now salvation is nearer to us than when we believed." The eternal, full, and final form of our salvation is nearer now than when we first believed in Christ.

The book of Hebrews says that angels are "ministering spirits, sent out to render service for the sake of those who will inherit salvation" (1:14). It also says that "Christ . . . having been offered once to bear the sins of many, shall appear a second time for salvation without reference to sin, to those who eagerly await Him" (9:28).

Our salvation is complete: past, present, and future. We can rejoice in the promise that "He who began a good work in [us] will perfect it until the day of Christ Jesus" (Phil. 1:6).

(b) The time of our salvation

Our salvation is "ready to be revealed in the last time" (1 Pet. 1:5). It hasn't yet been revealed in its fullness. "In the last time" refers to the final period of redemptive history when Christ returns.

(2) We inherit God

(a) As affirmed by Joshua

Joshua 13:32-33 says, "These are the territories which Moses apportioned for an inheritance in the plains of Moab, beyond the Jordan at Jericho to the east. But to the tribe of Levi, Moses did not give an inheritance; the Lord, the God of Israel, is their inheritance, as He had promised to them."

Because the priests were Levites, they did not receive land: the Lord Himself was their inheritance. They literally inherited God. That's an Old Testament principle, but I believe that it applies to Christians as well. First Peter 2:9 says that we, too, are "a royal priesthood."

(*b*) As affirmed by David and Asaph

> David said, "The Lord is the portion of my in-
> heritance" (Ps. 16:5). In Psalm 73:23-26 Asaph
> says, "I am continually with Thee; Thou hast
> taken hold of my right hand. With Thy counsel
> Thou wilt guide me, and afterward receive me
> to glory. Whom have I in heaven but Thee?
> And besides Thee, I desire nothing on earth.
> . . . God is the strength of my heart and my [in-
> heritance] forever."

(*c*) As affirmed by Jeremiah

> The prophet Jeremiah said, "'The Lord is my
> portion,' says my soul, 'Therefore I have hope
> in Him'" (Lam. 3:24).

That is a tremendous reality. We not only inherit
eternal salvation, but we also inherit God Himself
and will spend eternity in His presence.

(3) We inherit Christ

First John 3:2 says, "When [Christ] appears, we
shall be like Him, because we shall see Him just as
He is." Romans 8:17 says we are "heirs of God and
fellow heirs with Christ." Believers enter into an
eternal oneness with Him.

(4) We inherit the Holy Spirit

Ephesians 1:14 says that the Holy Spirit "is given
as a pledge of our inheritance." The Greek word
translated "pledge" (*arrabōn*) originally referred to
a down payment—money given to secure a purchase. Later it came to mean any sort of pledge.
One form of the word is used for an engagement
ring. The Holy Spirit is the resident guarantee of
our eternal inheritance.

Are You Looking Forward to Your Inheritance?

Many people are preoccupied with acquiring as much of this world's material goods as they can. But it seems unimportant to me whether we have much or little in this life. Ultimately we will leave it all behind. The priority is to love and serve Christ. He will grant us an eternal inheritance that far exceeds our wildest dreams. Paul said, "No eye has seen, no ear has heard, no mind has conceived what God has prepared for those who love him" (1 Cor. 2:9, NIV*).

Looking forward to our eternal inheritance will help us maintain a proper perspective on temporal things and motivate us to praise and adore God.

Lesson

Peter's doxology in 1 Peter 1:3-5 gives us additional insights into the nature of our inheritance so that we may more fully understand what God has done and therefore praise Him more intelligently. He specifies the source of our inheritance, the motive for our inheritance, the means by which we appropriate that inheritance, the nature of our inheritance, and the security of our inheritance.

I. THE SOURCE OF OUR INHERITANCE (v. 3a)

"Blessed be the God and Father of our Lord Jesus Christ."

The source of our inheritance is God, whom Peter described in four ways.

A. Our Blessed God

The Greek word translated "blessed" means "worthy of blessing, adoration, praise, or worship." God is worthy of blessing because of His gracious goodness.

We have seen that the main verb ("be") in verse 3 is implied rather than stated (see p. 9). The Greek construction assumes

* *New International Version.*

16

the action of blessing God. Peter was blessing God while instructing his readers to do the same.

B. Our Father God

1. A new identity for God

Identifying God as the "Father of our Lord Jesus Christ" gave Him a new identity in the Jewish mind. The most common Jewish prayers began, "Blessed art Thou, O God" (cf. Gen. 14:20; 24:27; Ex. 18:10), which the faithful recited several times daily. But they typically blessed God as Creator of all things (acknowledging His sovereign power) and Redeemer of His people from Egypt (acknowledging His saving power). We, however, bless God as the Father of our Lord Jesus Christ.

That was the Lord's instruction to the Samaritan woman in John 4:21-23: "Woman, believe Me, an hour is coming when neither in this mountain, nor in Jerusalem, shall you worship the Father. You worship that which you do not know; we worship that which we know, for salvation is from the Jews. But an hour is coming, and now is, when the true worshipers shall worship the Father in Spirit and truth; for such people the Father seeks to be His worshipers."

2. An affirmation of Christ's divinity

Peter did not refer to God as the Father of believers but as the Father of Christ. It is a trinitarian designation. In the gospels Jesus always addressed God as "Father" except when He was forsaken on the cross and cried out, "My God, My God, why hast Thou forsaken Me?" (Mark 15:34).

During the time of Jesus, a Jewish person never would have addressed God as "My Father." In the Old Testament He was called Father in a collective sense (e.g., Father of the nation of Israel, Deut. 32:6) but never in a personal, individual sense.

a) By Christ Himself

When Jesus identified God as His Father, He was not only breaking with Jewish tradition but was also claiming equality with God. In John 5:17 He says, "My Father is working until now, and I Myself am working," thereby equating His activities with the Father's. He also said, "I and the Father are one" (John 10:30)—a direct claim to equality. When Philip said, "Show us the Father," Jesus replied, "He who has seen Me has seen the Father" (John 14:9).

His enemies knew that when He claimed to be God's Son, Jesus was claiming equality with God. That is why they "took up stones . . . to stone Him. Jesus answered them, 'I showed you many good works from the Father; for which of them are you stoning Me?' The Jews answered Him, 'For a good work we do not stone You, but for blasphemy; and because You, being a man, make Yourself out to be God'" (John 10:31-33).

In John 17 Jesus again claims equality with God: "Father, the hour is come; glorify Thy Son, that the Son may glorify Thee. . . . Glorify Thou Me together with Thyself, Father, with the glory which I had with Thee before the world was" (vv. 1, 5).

In Matthew 11:27 Jesus says, "All things have been handed over to Me by My Father; and no one knows the Son, except the Father; nor does anyone know the Father, except the Son, and anyone to whom the Son wills to reveal Him." The Father and the Son know each other in an intimate way that no one else understands.

b) By Paul

(1) Ephesians 1:3—"Blessed be the God and Father of our Lord Jesus Christ."

(2) Ephesians 1:17—"The God of our Lord Jesus Christ, the Father of glory."

(3) 2 Corinthians 1:3—"Blessed be the God and Father of our Lord Jesus Christ."

c) By John

Second John 3 says, "Grace, mercy and peace will be with us, from God the Father and from Jesus Christ, the Son of the Father."

Whenever the New Testament speaks of God as "Father," it has primary reference to Him as the Father of the Lord Jesus Christ, who is equal in divine essence, and through whom the Father is known (John 14:6).

C. Our Redeemer God

Peter used the full redemptive name of Christ: the "Lord Jesus Christ" (1 Pet. 1:3). Commentator R. C. H. Lenski called that "a concentrated confession" (*The Interpretation of the Epistles of St. Peter, St. John and St. Jude* [Minneapolis: Augsburg, 1966], p. 30) because all that Scripture reveals about the redemptive work of God is embodied in that name. "Lord" speaks of His sovereign rulership; "Jesus" is the name of His incarnation; and "Christ" designates Him as the Messiah, the anointed King.

D. Our Personal God

The pronoun "our" ("our Lord Jesus Christ") in verse 3 is significant because it personalizes God. The divine Lord of the universe, the incarnate Savior, the anointed King and Messiah is not a distant deity to be appeased, but our personal Lord and Savior.

Being one with Christ means we are also one with the Father (John 17:21-23). First Corinthians 6:17 says, "The one who joins himself to the Lord is one spirit with Him." Jesus said, "He who overcomes, I will grant to him to sit with Me on My throne, as I also overcame and sat down with My Father on His throne" (Rev. 3:21). We share in Christ's throne and in the Father's throne as well. We will enjoy eternal intimacy with God the Father, Son, and Holy Spirit.

Conclusion

We bless God because He is the source of our inheritance. If we had earned our inheritance by our own efforts or by any other means, we wouldn't bless God. But God gave it to us solely on the basis of the redemption He accomplished through the Lord Jesus Christ. He made us His children by choosing us "according to [His] foreknowledge . . . by the sanctifying work of the Spirit" (1 Pet. 1:2), thereby qualifying us to receive such an inheritance.

I believe it to be a sin of massive proportions to live a thankless life. We should always be praising, blessing, adoring, honoring, extolling, and worshiping God for our eternal inheritance. Are you thankful for your inheritance?

Focusing on the Facts

1. What reminders did Peter give his readers (1 Pet. 1:3; see pp. 8-9)?
2. According to 1 Peter 2:21-23, how did Jesus respond to persecution (see p. 8)?
3. Identify three aspects of our inheritance mentioned in Ephesians (Eph. 1:10-18; see p. 10).
4. Define "inheritance" as used in 1 Peter 1:4 (see p. 10).
5. What inheritance did God promise to Abraham and his descendants (Gen. 17:8; see p. 11)?
6. What admonition does Paul give the Colossian believers in Colossians 3:2 (see p. 12)?
7. Define "salvation" as used in 1 Peter 1:5 (see p. 13).
8. What are the three tenses of salvation? Give an example of each (see pp. 13-14).
9. What does the phrase "ready to be revealed in the last time" mean (1 Pet. 1:5; see p. 14)?
10. Define "pledge" as used in Ephesians 1:14 (see p. 15).
11. In what four ways did Peter describe the source of our inheritance (1 Pet. 1:3; see pp. 16-19)?
12. Define "blessed" as used in 1 Peter 1:3 (see p. 16).
13. How did Jewish people typically identify God in their prayers (see p. 17)?

14. When Jesus identified God as His Father, He was not only breaking with Jewish tradition but was also claiming _____ with God (see p. 18).
15. What does the name "Lord Jesus Christ" signify (see p. 19)?
16. What is the significance of the pronoun "our" in 1 Peter 1:3 (see p. 19)?

Pondering the Principles

1. As Christians, our hearts should be continually filled with praise toward God. However, sometimes amid difficult circumstances we lose sight of His blessings and the inheritance that is ours in Christ. At such times it is important to stimulate praise by reflecting on His grace and mercy as revealed in Scripture. A good way to do that is to read the book of Ephesians, noting everything that is ours "in Christ." For example, "Blessed be the God and Father of our Lord Jesus Christ, who has blessed us with every spiritual blessing in the heavenly places *in Christ*" (Eph. 1:3, emphasis added). The phrase "in Christ" occurs many times in Ephesians, which will trigger praise to God for many things.

2. Adoring God for our eternal inheritance is largely a matter of proper spiritual priorities. If you're consumed with material gain, you will not appreciate the value of spiritual blessings. Jesus said, "You cannot serve both God and Money" (Matt. 6:24, NIV). He also said, "Seek first [the Father's] kingdom and His righteousness; and all [the necessities of life] shall be added to you" (Matt. 6:33). Are your priorities in order? Perhaps you are pursuing things that need to be set aside. If so, turn from them and seek the Lord's wisdom and grace to enable you to worship and adore Him wholeheartedly.

2
Adoring God
for Our Eternal Inheritance—Part 2

Outline

Introduction
A. The Passage
B. The Principle
C. The Problem

Review
I. The Source of Our Inheritance (v. 3*a*)

Lesson
II. The Motive of Our Inheritance (v. 3*b*)
   A. The Affirmation of God's Mercy
   B. The Description of God's Mercy
      1. It tempers God's justice
      2. It addresses man's condition
      3. It complements God's grace
      4. It reveals God's compassion
III. The Means of Our Inheritance (v. 3*c*)
   A. The Nature of Our New Birth
      1. We were born as sinful creatures
      2. We were born again as new creations
   B. The Result of Our New Birth
      1. The nature of our hope
      2. The basis of our hope (v. 3*e*)
IV. The Nature of Our Inheritance (v. 4*a*)
   A. It Is Imperishable
      1. Its definition
      2. Its secular usage

B. It Is Undefiled
C. It Is Unfading
V. The Security of Our Inheritance (vv. 4b-5)
  A. Our Inheritance Is Protected for Us (v. 4b)
    1. The nature of its protection
    2. The place of its protection
  B. We Are Protected for Our Inheritance (v. 5)
    1. The fact of our protection
    2. The means of our protection
    3. The results of our protection

Conclusion

Introduction

A. The Passage

First Peter 1:3-5 says, "Blessed be the God and Father of our Lord Jesus Christ, who according to His great mercy has caused us to be born again to a living hope through the resurrection of Jesus Christ from the dead, to obtain an inheritance which is imperishable and undefiled and will not fade away, reserved in heaven for you, who are protected by the power of God through faith for a salvation ready to be revealed in the last time."

B. The Principle

In that passage the apostle Peter extolled the wonder of our salvation—our "inheritance" (v. 4)—which will be fully revealed when Jesus comes. Such a wonderful blessing should continually motivate every Christian to worship and adore God for the richness of His grace.

C. The Problem

It's appalling to see how indifferent we can be to the reality of our salvation, especially when considering the fact that in heaven we'll be joined by the holy angels in expressing eternal, undiminished praise to God for His redemption of mankind. Yet now we often struggle with apathy.

What a commentary it is on our sinfulness that we have to be exhorted to praise God for our eternal inheritance! That should be the incessant occupation of our hearts. I pray that our study of 1 Peter 1:3-5 will stir us to praise and adore God as we should.

Review

Peter's doxology gives five aspects of our eternal inheritance that should elicit praise to God: its source, motive, means, nature, and security.

I. THE SOURCE OF OUR INHERITANCE (v. 3*a*; see pp. 16-20)

"Blessed be the God and Father of our Lord Jesus Christ."

Lesson

II. THE MOTIVE OF OUR INHERITANCE (v. 3*b*)

"According to His great mercy."

God's mercy motivated Him to grant us salvation.

A. The Affirmation of God's Mercy

1. Titus 3:5—"[God] saved us, not on the basis of deeds which we have done in righteousness, but according to His mercy, by the washing of regeneration and renewing by the Holy Spirit."

2. Ephesians 2:4-5—"God, being rich in mercy, because of His great love with which He loved us, even when we were dead in our transgressions, made us alive together with Christ (by grace you have been saved)."

B. The Description of God's Mercy

1. It tempers God's justice

   The Puritan writer Thomas Watson said, "Mercy sweetens all God's other attributes. God's holiness without mercy, and his justice without mercy were terrible. When the water was bitter, and Israel could not drink, Moses cast a tree into the waters, and then they were made sweet. How bitter and dreadful were the other attributes of God, did not mercy sweeten them! Mercy sets God's power [at] work to help us; it makes his justice become our friend; it shall avenge our quarrels" (*A Body of Divinity* [Edinburgh: Banner of Truth Trust, 1978], p. 94).

2. It addresses man's condition

   God's mercy focuses on the pitiful condition of mankind. The blind beggar Bartimaeus cried out, saying, "Jesus, Son of David, have mercy on me!" (Mark 10:47).

   Sinners need someone to show mercy and compassion on them because they are dead in trespasses, enslaved to sin, unable to help themselves, and cursed to eternal damnation. Their minds and desires are corrupt, deceitful, and wicked. They desperately need mercy, and the good news of the gospel is that God is merciful and compassionate toward repentant sinners.

3. It complements God's grace

   Mercy addresses man's sinful condition; grace addresses the guilt that caused his condition. Mercy changes his condition; grace changes his position or standing before God's law. Mercy takes him from misery to glory; grace takes him from guilt to acquittal.

4. It reveals God's compassion

   There is nothing desirable within us that would motivate God to save us. He does so because He is compassionate and merciful and because He grieves over our misery.

a) As seen in Christ's healing ministry

The healing ministry of Jesus demonstrated God's compassion for man's plight. He could have proved His deity in a myriad of other ways, but He chose to relieve human suffering.

b) As seen throughout Scripture

(1) Exodus 34:6—"The Lord, the Lord God, [is] merciful and gracious, long suffering, and abundant in goodness and truth" (KJV*).

(2) Psalm 108:4—"[God's] mercy is great above the heavens" (KJV). It is voluminous and sufficient for any situation.

(3) Micah 7:18—"[God] delighteth in mercy" (KJV).

(4) Lamentations 3:22-23—"It is because of the Lord's mercies that we are not consumed, because his compassions fail not. They are new every morning; great is thy faithfulness" (KJV). That God permits us to live at all is a testimony to His mercy.

(5) Romans 9:15—"I will have mercy on whom I have mercy." The sovereignty of God governs the exercise of His mercy. The gift of salvation is perhaps the greatest example of His mercy and compassion.

(6) 2 Corinthians 1:3—"Blessed be the God and Father of our Lord Jesus Christ, the Father of mercies and God of all comfort."

God's saving mercy is free, abundant, and eternal. What greater motivation could there be to glorify Him with pure lives and praise on our lips?

*King James Version.

III. THE MEANS OF OUR INHERITANCE (v. 3c)

"[He] caused us to be born again to a living hope through the resurrection of Jesus Christ from the dead."

A. The Nature of Our New Birth

The new birth is the means by which God's mercy eliminates the wretchedness and misery of man's sinful condition.

1. We were born as sinful creatures

   a) Ephesians 2:1, 3, 12—"You were dead in your trespasses and sins . . . indulging the desires of the flesh and of the mind, and were by nature children of wrath . . . separate from Christ . . . having no hope and without God in the world."

   We were born utterly enslaved to sin. The depth of our depravity necessitated a new birth.

   b) Jeremiah 13:23—"Can the Ethiopian change his skin or the leopard his spots? Then you also can do good who are accustomed to do evil." Sinful people cannot change their condition; they must be transformed by the Holy Spirit.

2. We were born again as new creations

   a) By identifying with Christ

   Paul said, "If any man is in Christ, he is a new creature; the old things passed away; behold, new things have come" (2 Cor. 5:17).

   Romans 8:17 says that believers are "heirs of God and fellow heirs with Christ." We are new creations and recipients of an eternal inheritance.

Will You Inherit Heaven or Hell?

All believers receive the eternal inheritance that God has promised to His children, but unbelievers also receive an inheritance: the wrath of God and eternal flames (Matt. 25:41-46; Eph. 2:3). That, too, is an inescapable, eternal inheritance. Which one will you receive? The choice is yours.

When you submit your life to Christ, you are born again. That means the Holy Spirit transforms you by indwelling you and giving you new life, perspectives, priorities, and desires. You become Christ-centered rather than self-centered.

b) By receiving God's Word

Peter said, "You have been born again not of seed which is perishable but imperishable, that is, through the living and abiding word of God. . . . This is the word which was preached to you" (1 Pet. 1:23, 25). God's Spirit working through God's Word activates our faith. That results in saving faith, which brings about the new birth.

c) By trusting in Christ

(1) A hindrance to trusting in Christ

Jesus discussed the new birth with Nicodemus, a highly esteemed ruler of the Jewish people and a leading scholar. Such men typically lived by an external code of religious conduct, apart from true love for God (cf. John 8:42).

As entrenched as Nicodemus was in his beliefs, he probably expected Jesus to tell him to add something to his religious beliefs so that they would be more complete. Instead Jesus said, "Unless one is born again, he cannot see the kingdom of God" (John 3:3).

In effect Jesus was saying, "Nicodemus, despite how far you've progressed in your religion, you have to start all over again." Nicodemus had to shed his legalistic religion before he could understand and experience God's redeeming grace.

In Matthew 21:31 Jesus says to the Jewish leaders, "Truly I say to you that the tax-gatherers and harlots will get into the kingdom of God before you." Those people were closer to God's kingdom than the religious leaders because they had no religion to shed.

Nicodemus and his fellow Jewish leaders believed they could be saved by their own works. But salvation comes only to those who realize their inability to save themselves. We must turn to Jesus Christ, who alone has the power and authority to forgive sins and redeem sinners.

(2) An illustration of trusting in Christ

Jesus gave Nicodemus a Jewish illustration of the new birth: "As Moses lifted up the serpent in the wilderness, even so must the Son of Man be lifted up; that whoever believes may in Him have eternal life. For God so loved the world, that He gave His only begotten Son, that whoever believes in Him should not perish, but have eternal life" (John 3:14-16).

Jesus drew His illustration from the time of Israel's wanderings when they spoke against God and Moses, saying, "'Why have you brought us up out of Egypt to die in the wilderness? For there is no food and water, and we loathe this miserable food.'

"And the Lord sent fiery serpents among the people and they bit the people, so that many people of Israel died. So the people came to Moses and said, 'We have sinned, because we have spoken against the Lord and you; intercede with the

Lord, that He may remove the serpents from us.'
And Moses interceded for the people.

"Then the Lord said to Moses, 'Make a fiery serpent, and set it on a standard; and it shall come about, that everyone who is bitten, when he looks at it, he shall live.' And Moses made a bronze serpent and set it on the standard; and it came about, that if a serpent bit any man, when he looked to the bronze serpent, he lived" (Num. 21:5-9).

The people acknowledged their sin by looking at that serpent, and then they received deliverance from their physical distress. Jesus used that illustration to show Nicodemus that the new birth would come by turning from sin and looking to Himself, for He would hang on a cross to provide spiritual deliverance.

Nicodemus had to acknowledge that his self-righteous religion was nothing more than a snake bite from which he needed healing.

It is appropriate that Satan, the author of all false religion, is called "the serpent of old" (Rev. 20:2).

Have You Been Born Again?

The new birth is vital: it is the only way we can receive the mercy of God and our eternal inheritance, and it comes only through faith in Jesus Christ. In Him we are "born again to a living hope through the resurrection of Jesus Christ from the dead" (1 Pet. 1:3).

The Bible has much to say about the new birth.

- It is accomplished by the will of God, not man (John 1:13).
- It is the work of the Holy Spirit (John 3:5; Titus 3:5).
- It is activated through God's Word (1 Pet. 1:23).
- It makes us new creations in Christ (2 Cor. 5:17; James 1:18).

The Puritan theologian Stephen Charnock said that the new birth "is a universal change of the whole man. . . . It is as large in re-

31

newing, as sin was in defacing" (*The Doctrine of Regeneration* [Grand Rapids: Baker, 1980 reprint], p. 103).

The new birth is the only solution to the unbeliever's enslavement to sin and alienation from God. Have you been born again?

B. The Result of Our New Birth

The result of our inheritance is a hope that is perpetually alive.

1. The nature of our hope

All hope apart from Jesus Christ is dying or dead. At best, men's hopes and dreams die with them. Paul said, "If we have hoped in Christ in this life only, we are of all men most to be pitied" (1 Cor. 15:19). Christians are to be pitied if Jesus is not the living, resurrected Lord.

a) It rests on God's integrity

The Christian's hope is an eternal hope that rests on God's ability to fulfill all His promises (cf. Jer. 32:27; Rom. 8:28). Our hope is in a "new heavens and a new earth, in which righteousness dwells" (2 Pet. 3:13).

b) It anticipates perfect fellowship

Paul said, "To me, to live is Christ, and to die is gain" (Phil. 1:21). Death is gain to believers because it ushers us into Christ's presence where our hope becomes reality. Only then can we enjoy full and unhindered fellowship with God, Christ, the Holy Spirit, angels, and saints. We will serve God perfectly, experience the glory of heaven, and enjoy our eternal inheritance in perfect holiness and freedom from sin.

2. The basis of our hope (v. 3e)

Our hope is based on the resurrection of Jesus Christ from the dead. Consequently we need never fear the grave. William Gurnall observed that hope is the saint's covering, wherein he wraps himself when he lays his body down to sleep in the grave" (cf. *The Christian in Complete Armour*, vol. 2 [London: Banner of Truth, 1964 reprint], pp. 170-71).

a) As affirmed by Jesus

Jesus said, "Because I live, you shall live also" (John 14:19). In John 11:25 He says, "I am the resurrection and the life; he who believes in Me shall live even if he dies." He then substantiated His claim by raising Lazarus from the dead (John 11:43-44).

b) As affirmed by Paul

Paul said, "If Christ has not been raised, your faith is worthless; you are still in your sins" (1 Cor. 15:17). The resurrection is the crown of Christ's atoning work. By His death and resurrection He bore the sins of the world, satisfied the righteousness of God, conquered death, and gave us a living hope. Those riches are ours through the new birth.

IV. THE NATURE OF OUR INHERITANCE (v. 4*a*)

"To obtain an inheritance which is imperishable and undefiled and will not fade away."

A. It Is Imperishable

1. Its definition

The Greek word translated "imperishable" (*aphthartos*) means incorruptible and unable to decay.

2. Its secular usage

Aphthartos was used in secular Greek to describe a land unravaged by an invading army (*Linguistic Key to the Greek New Testament*, p. 744). Our inheritance cannot be ravaged or violated by the enemy of our souls.

a) The Old Testament parallel

> God said to Moses, "I have come down to deliver [Israel] from the power of the Egyptians, and to bring them up from that land to a good and spacious land, to a land flowing with milk and honey, to the place of the Canaanite" (Ex. 3:8). That was their earthly inheritance, but many times it was plundered by invading armies. By contrast, our spiritual inheritance will never be ravaged, plundered, or devastated.

b) The New Testament principle

> Jesus said, "Do not lay up for yourselves treasures upon earth, where moth and rust destroy, and where thieves break in and steal. But lay up for yourselves treasures in heaven, where neither moth nor rust destroys, and where thieves do not break in or steal" (Matt. 6:19-20).

> Our treasure is secure in heaven. You may think you are secure on earth because you have bank accounts, stocks, and bonds, but all such things are perishable. Even if they aren't lost or stolen, you will leave them behind when you die. But your spiritual inheritance is eternally secure.

B. It Is Undefiled

> The Greek word translated "undefiled" (*amiantos*) speaks of something unpolluted or unstained by sin, evil, or decay. Everything in this world is defiled by sin and is defective—everything will fail. Paul said, "The creation was subjected to futility . . . in hope that the creation itself also will be set free from its slavery to corruption into the freedom of the glory of the children of God. For we know that the whole creation groans and suffers the pains of childbirth together until now. . . . But also we ourselves . . . groan within ourselves, waiting eagerly for our adoption as sons, the redemption of our body" (Rom. 8:20-23).

Where Is Your Treasure?

Paul viewed his earthly inheritance as useless rubbish compared to the surpassing value of knowing Jesus Christ (Phil. 3:8). Above all else he wanted the righteousness that comes through faith in Him (v. 9). That's an imperishable inheritance.

Where is your treasure? Are you storing it up in heaven to add to the joy of your eternal salvation? Or are you foolishly storing it up on earth where it can be defiled (Matt. 6:19-20)?

C. It Is Unfading

"Will not fade away" (Gk., *amarantos*) speaks of something that is unfading. It was used of flowers, and in 1 Peter 1:4 suggests a supernatural beauty that time does not impair (*Linguistic Key to the Greek New Testament*, p. 744). Peter also used *amarantos* to speak of the unfading crown of glory that elders will receive when the Chief Shepherd appears (1 Pet. 5:4).

The kingdom of heaven is timeless and sinless, where nothing ever perishes, fades away, or is defiled. That is cause for great rejoicing and praising God, especially when considering the corrupting influence sin has on our world.

V. THE SECURITY OF OUR INHERITANCE (vv. 4*b*-5)

A. Our Inheritance Is Protected for Us (v. 4*b*)

"Reserved in heaven for you."

1. The nature of its protection

We need never fear the loss of our inheritance because it is reserved in heaven for us. No one can steal or plunder it. The Greek word translated "reserved" means "to guard." Its perfect passive participle form in the Greek text indicates an inheritance that already exists, is presently being guarded, and will continually be guarded (*Linguistic Key to the Greek New Testament*, p. 744).

2. The place of its protection

Our inheritance is guarded in heaven—the safest place possible. It is in heaven that "neither moth nor rust destroys, and where thieves do not break in or steal" (Matt. 6:20), and "nothing [is] unclean and no one who practices abomination and lying, shall ever [enter], but only those whose names are written in the Lamb's book of life" (Rev. 21:27).

Revelation 22:14-15 says, "Blessed are those who wash their robes, that they may have the right to the tree of life, and may enter by the gates into the city. Outside are the dogs and the sorcerers and the immoral persons and the murderers and the idolaters, and everyone who loves and practices lying." Heaven will never know invasion or the spoiling of its treasure. Therefore our inheritance is eternally secure.

B. We Are Protected for Our Inheritance (v. 5)

"Who are protected by the power of God through faith for a salvation ready to be revealed in the last time."

1. The fact of our protection

Not only is our inheritance protected, but we ourselves are protected as well. Many believe a Christian can lose his or her salvation, but 1 Peter says we are protected from any such loss.

The Greek word translated "protected" is a military term indicating a guard. Its present tense in the Greek text indicates continuous action, which implies a need for continuous protection in our spiritual warfare with the forces of Satan.

2. The means of our protection

a) Persevering power

We are continually being guarded by God's omnipotent, sovereign power, and that is the guarantee of our final victory (*Linguistic Key to the Greek New Testament*, p. 744).

Even Satan himself cannot condemn us because God has declared us righteous (Rom. 8:33), and "if God is for us, who [can successfully be] against us?" (Rom. 8:31). There is no higher court than God, and He has acquitted us and placed His Spirit within us to insure ultimate victory. Philippians 1:6 says, "He who began a good work in you will perfect it until the day of Christ Jesus." He "is able to keep you from stumbling, and to make you stand in the presence of His glory blameless with great joy" (Jude 24).

We needn't fear the loss of our inheritance. Rather, we should continually rejoice in God's great mercy and grace.

b) Persevering faith

Another important guarantee of our inheritance is our persevering faith. It is not something we generate on our own. God saved us by granting us the ability to believe the gospel (Eph. 2:8-9; Phil. 1:29), and He continues to energize our faith so that we continue to believe.

R. C. H. Lenski said, "Faith is kindled and is preserved and made strong by grace alone. Grace alone reaches into the heart and the soul and works spiritual effects" (*The Interpretation of the Epistles of St. Peter, St. John and St. Jude* [Minneapolis: Augsburg, 1966], p. 35).

Daniel is an example of God's power and man's faith working together. God shut the lions' mouths to protect Daniel, and Daniel exercised his great faith (Dan. 6:19-23).

3. The results of our protection

Peter described our inheritance as "a salvation ready to be revealed in the last time" (1 Pet. 1:5). We have experienced only a taste of our inheritance, but its fullness is guaranteed when Christ comes in all His glory.

Conclusion

God has given us an eternal and glorious inheritance. No matter what our circumstances might be, the reality of that inheritance should cause us to praise and adore God, living each day for the sole purpose of glorifying Him.

Focusing on the Facts

1. What motivated God to give us an inheritance (1 Pet. 1:3; see p. 25)?
2. In what way does God's mercy address man's sinful condition (see p. 26)?
3. Contrast God's mercy with His grace (see p. 26).
4. Which attributes of God are mentioned in Exodus 34:6 (see p. 27)?
5. What does Romans 9:15 teach us about God's mercy (see p. 27)?
6. The gift of _____ is perhaps the greatest example of God's mercy and compassion (see p. 27).
7. What is the means of our inheritance (1 Pet. 1:3; see p. 28)?
8. What does Ephesians 2 teach us about the spiritual condition of mankind prior to salvation (see p. 28)?
9. What is the role of God's Word in the new birth (1 Pet. 1:23, 25; see p. 29)?
10. Why did Jesus say tax collectors and prostitutes would enter the kingdom of God before the Jewish religious leaders (Matt. 21:31; see p. 30)?
11. What illustration did Jesus use to explain the new birth to Nicodemus (John 3:15; Num. 21:9; see pp. 30-31)?
12. Identify four aspects of the new birth (see p. 31).
13. Explain the nature of the Christian's hope (1 Pet. 1:3; see p. 32).
14. What is the basis of the Christian's hope (1 Pet. 1:3; see pp. 32-33)?
15. Define "imperishable" as used in 1 Peter 1:4. How was it used in secular Greek (see p. 33)?
16. Define "undefiled" as used in 1 Peter 1:4 (see p. 34).

17. What did Peter mean by an inheritance that "will not fade away" (1 Pet. 1:4; see p. 35)?
18. What guarantees do Christians have that they will receive their eternal inheritance (1 Pet. 1:4-5; see pp. 35-37)?

Pondering the Principles

1. We have seen how God's mercy or lovingkindness motivated Him to give us an eternal inheritance (see pp. 25-27). In Psalm 136 the psalmist reflects on God's mercy as it applied to Israel. Read that psalm, noting the manifestations of mercy that relate to your life. Then spend time in prayer thanking God for the wonder of His great mercy.

2. Christians are born of the imperishable seed of God's Word (1 Pet. 1:23). That means the Holy Spirit energized the preaching of the Word to activate our faith in Christ. Beyond that, He also uses the Word to purify us (Heb. 4:12-13) and equip us for spiritual service (2 Tim. 3:16-17). That's why prayer and Bible study are so crucial to our spiritual life. Prayer keeps us in touch with the source of our spiritual resources, and Bible study helps us live each day to God's glory. Have you cultivated the discipline of daily prayer and Bible study? If so, guard that time carefully. If not, begin to do so today. Find someone with whom you can share what you are learning and who will pray with you and hold you accountable for your devotional time.

3. Many people struggle with a profound sense of hopelessness. They know they cannot control their circumstances or destiny, and they sense that ultimately everything will be lost to death. But Christians have a living, eternal hope because we know the resurrected Lord. That is our message to people who are alienated from God and without hope (Eph. 2:12). We must be faithful to proclaim it. Pray that God will use you today to communicate His love and hope to others, and look for opportunities to do so.

39

3
The Joy of Salvation—Part 1

Outline

Introduction
A. The Theme of Joy
B. The Threats to Joy
  1. Sin
  2. Persecution
C. The Companions of Joy

Lesson
I. A Protected Inheritance (v. 6a)
  A. The Joy of Our Inheritance
  B. The Nature of Our Inheritance
  C. The Proof of Our Inheritance
    1. The resurrection of Jesus Christ
    2. The coming of the Holy Spirit
     a) He is the source of joy
     b) He is the guarantee of our inheritance
  D. The Results of Our Inheritance
    1. A proper perspective
    2. A realistic anticipation
II. A Proved Faith (vv. 6-7a)
  A. The Principles of Proved Faith (v. 6)
  B. The Products of Proved Faith (v. 7a)
    1. The analogy
    2. The application
    3. The illustrations
     a) Jesus
     b) Abraham
     c) Job
     d) The Israelites
     e) The apostles

C. The Preciousness of Proved Faith

Conclusion

Introduction

A. The Theme of Joy

First Peter 1:6-10 shows the direct correlation between salvation and joy, mentioning *salvation* three times (vv. 5, 9, 10) and *joy* twice in the same context (vv. 6, 8). Joy is shown to be a result of salvation, so all believers should experience joy.

B. The Threats to Joy

1. Sin

When we harbor unconfessed sin, we forfeit our joy. It can be restored only by confession and repentance. David, after acknowledging his terrible sins of adultery and murder, said, "Restore to me the joy of Thy salvation" (Ps. 51:12).

2. Persecution

God uses persecution to test our faith and to produce joy in us (James 1:2). However, it is possible to lose our perspective and allow trials to rob us of our joy. The Christians to whom Peter wrote were facing that possibility because of the severe persecution resulting from the burning of Rome.

They were being slandered as evildoers (1 Pet. 2:12) and were suffering unjustly (vv. 19-20). Peter exhorted them to exercise endurance and patience because they had been "called for this purpose, since Christ also suffered for [them], leaving [them] an example . . . to follow in His steps" (v. 21).

Apparently they were also being insulted, but Peter instructed them not to respond by retaliating (1 Pet. 3:9). In verses 14-17 Peter says, "Even if you should suffer for the sake of righteousness, you are blessed. And do not fear their intimidation, and do not be troubled, but sanctify Christ as Lord in your hearts, always being ready to make a defense to everyone who asks you to give an account for the hope that is in you, yet with gentleness and reverence; and keep a good conscience so that in the thing in which you are slandered, those who revile your good behavior in Christ may be put to shame. For it is better, if God should will it so, that you suffer for doing what is right rather than for doing what is wrong."

He went on to say, "Since Christ has suffered in the flesh, arm yourselves also with the same purpose. . . . Do not be surprised at the fiery ordeal among you, which comes upon you for your testing, as though some strange thing were happening to you; but to the degree that you share the sufferings of Christ, keep on rejoicing; so that also at the revelation of His glory, you may rejoice with exultation.

"If you are reviled for the name of Christ, you are blessed, because the Spirit of glory and of God rests upon you. . . . If anyone suffers as a Christian, let him not feel ashamed, but in that name let him glorify God. . . . After you have suffered for a little while, the God of all grace, who called you to His eternal glory in Christ, will Himself perfect, confirm, strengthen and establish you" (1 Pet. 4:1, 12-14, 16; 5:10).

Because they were experiencing such difficulties, Peter reminded his readers of the blessedness of their salvation and the joy that should result from it.

C. The Companions of Joy

When persecution or other trials rob us of our joy, we can regain it by focusing on the elements of joy Peter gives in 1 Peter 1:6-9: "In this you greatly rejoice, even though now for a little while, if necessary, you have been distressed by various trials, that the proof of your faith, being more precious than gold which is perishable, even though tested by fire, may be found to result in praise and glory and honor at the revelation of Jesus Christ; and though you have not seen Him, you love Him, and though you do not see Him now, but believe in Him, you greatly rejoice with joy inexpressible and full of glory, obtaining as the outcome of your faith the salvation of your souls."

In that passage we see joy linked with faith, hope, and love. Joy is not merely a shallow, fleeting emotion. It is a gift from God grounded in the gospel of Christ and the ministry of the Holy Spirit.

That is the primary difference between joy and happiness. Happiness is the result of positive circumstances; joy is the result of the Spirit's ministry in an individual's life who has a proper relationship with God through Jesus Christ.

Lesson

First Peter 1:6-9 identifies five elements that help us retain or regain the joy of our salvation in the midst of trials: a protected inheritance, a proved faith, a promised honor, a personal fellowship, and a present deliverance.

I. A PROTECTED INHERITANCE (v. 6a)

"In this you greatly rejoice."

A. The Joy of Our Inheritance

The Greek word translated "greatly rejoice" (*agalliaō*) is an expressive word. Jesus used it when He said, "Be exceedingly glad" (Matt. 5:12, KJV). It is a much stronger word than *chairō*, the usual Greek word for "rejoice."

Agalliaō describes one who is happy in a profound spiritual sense rather than in a temporal or circumstantial sense. It "appears to be used always with the connotation of a 'religious' joy, a joy which springs from the contemplation of God or of the salvation which comes from God" (*Linguistic Key to the Greek New Testament*, p. 745). Peter's use of the Greek present middle voice carries the idea of a continual, exuberant joy and gladness.

B. The Nature of Our Inheritance

The phrase "in this" refers back to verses 3-5: "Blessed be the God and Father of our Lord Jesus Christ, who according to His great mercy has caused us to be born again to a living hope through the resurrection of Jesus Christ from the dead, to obtain an inheritance which is imperishable and undefiled and will not fade away, reserved in heaven for you, who are protected by the power of God through faith for a salvation ready to be revealed in the last time."

Our protected inheritance is the first element in salvation joy.

C. The Proof of Our Inheritance

1. The resurrection of Jesus Christ

There was a time when joy eluded the disciples. Jesus said to them, "A little while, and you will no longer behold Me; and again a little while, and you will see Me. . . . Truly, truly, I say to you, that you will weep and lament, but the world will rejoice; you will be sorrowful, but your sorrow will be turned to joy.

"Whenever a woman is in travail she has sorrow, because her hour has come; but when she gives birth to the child, she remembers the anguish no more, for joy that a child has been born into the world. Therefore you, too, now have sorrow; but I will see you again, and your heart will rejoice, and no one takes your joy away from you" (John 16:16, 20-22).

The disciples' dark hour came when Jesus was in the grave. He had promised to prepare a place for them and to return to take them there (John 14:3), but His death seemed to nullify His promise. When the disciples witnessed the resurrected Lord, however, their sorrow turned to joy because they knew His promise of eternal life had been verified.

2. The coming of the Holy Spirit

  a) He is the source of joy

  I believe Jesus had both His resurrection and the coming of the Spirit in mind in John 16. Even after Christ's resurrection, the disciples didn't fully understand God's plan for Christ or for them because they had not yet received the resident Holy Spirit. It was the Spirit who would bring understanding and joy (Gal. 5:22).

  b) He is the guarantee of our inheritance

  Paul said, "We who were the first to hope in Christ should be to the praise of His glory. In Him, you also, after listening to the message of truth, the gospel of your salvation—having also believed, you were sealed in Him with the Holy Spirit of promise, who is given as a pledge of our inheritance" (Eph. 1:12-14).

Our joy is not subject to circumstances because it is based on the historical fact of the resurrection (Rom. 10:9) and the present reality of the indwelling Spirit (Rom. 8:9), who is the guarantee that God will fulfill His promise of an eternal inheritance. That's why we can "rejoice in hope of the glory of God" (Rom. 5:2; 12:12, KJV).

D. The Results of Our Inheritance

  1. A proper perspective

  When we experience trials, we need not succumb to discouragement or despair. We can look beyond this mundane, temporal world to the glory of the inheritance that awaits us in heaven.

  That is not an artificial or unrealistic perspective. It does not mean we pretend to have joy by denying pain and suffering. Your troubles may never cease in this life, but God promises to provide grace, peace, and joy to sustain you in the midst of them. Focusing on your inheritance is an important factor in experiencing His provisions.

Imagine you are riding a train as it passes through a mountain range. To your left is a very steep hill that casts its dark shadow over the side of the train. On your right, stretching as far as the eye can see, are magnificent valleys, meadows, streams, and lakes.

Which view do you prefer? Some choose to stare at the dark mountains of life. Others drink in the beauty of their hope, wealth, and security in Christ. If you are a Christian struggling with heavy burdens, guilt, unfulfilled aspirations, or broken resolutions, perhaps you need a change of perspective. Remember the glorious, protected, eternal inheritance that awaits you!

2. A realistic anticipation

Christian joy is largely the joy of anticipation—looking forward to the fulfillment of God's promises. We anticipate joy in a temporal sense when we look forward to a vacation or the purchase of a new home or car. How much more should we rejoice in anticipation of our heavenly inheritance?

Quite often the temporal things that we anticipate prove to be less than expected, but not so with our eternal inheritance. It will far exceed our expectations, but the anticipation is enough to give us joy now.

II. A PROVED FAITH (vv. 6-7a)

Our joy is one of anticipation, but it is also born out of present trials. It does not come *in spite* of trouble but *because* of trouble. God brings trials to test and prove the validity of our faith. When we pass the tests, we experience great joy.

That is contrary to the belief that trials and persecution can only rob Christians of their joy. The easiest way to lose your Christian joy is to doubt your salvation, because then you have no reason for looking to the future with joy. However, proved faith eliminates doubt, thereby bringing joy.

A. The Principles of Proved Faith (v. 6)

"In this you greatly rejoice, even though now for a little while, if necessary, you have been distressed by various trials."

Verse 6 is a summary of the parameters within which God works to test and perfect our faith. They should encourage us whenever we face difficult circumstances.

1. Trials don't last—"For a little while."

   Trouble is temporary and transient. It is relegated to this life.

2. Trials serve a purpose—"If necessary."

   Our troubles can teach us humility, wean us from worldly things, focus our attention on heaven, reveal our true priorities, increase our appreciation for God's blessings, enable us to help others, develop enduring strength of character, chasten us for sin, increase our sense of dependency on God, purge us for greater usefulness, and produce joy.

   First Peter 5:10 says, "After you have suffered a little while, the God of all grace, who called you to His eternal glory in Christ, will Himself perfect, confirm, strengthen and establish you."

3. Trials bring pain—"You have been distressed."

   In addition to physical anguish, trouble can bring mental anguish such as sadness, disappointment, or anxiety.

4. Trials come in many forms—"By various trials."

   Commentator William Barclay said, "The Christian for the moment may well have to undergo various trials. The Greek is *poikilos*, which literally means many-coloured. Peter uses that word only one other time and it is to describe the grace of God (1 Pet. 4:10). Our troubles may be many-coloured, but so is the grace of God; there is no colour in the human situation that grace cannot match. There is a grace to match every trial and there is no trial without its grace" (*The Letters of James and Peter*, rev. ed. [Philadelphia: Westminster, 1976], p. 177).

5. Trouble needn't diminish joy—"In this you greatly rejoice."

We can rejoice in the midst of troubles when we understand God's purpose for testing our faith.

B. The Products of Proved Faith (v. 7a)

"That the proof of your faith, being more precious than gold which is perishable, even though tested by fire."

If your faith is never tested, you cannot know whether it is genuine. Therefore it is for our own benefit that God tests our faith. He already knows if we are genuine because He knows our hearts. He wants us to have confidence in the quality of our faith.

1. The analogy

Peter used the analogy of an assayer or goldsmith to illustrate the purging process. In his analogy "fire" symbolizes trials, and "gold" symbolizes our faith. "Proof" is the final outcome of the assaying process—the tested, pure metal. A goldsmith uses fire to burn away the dross and end up with pure gold. In the same way, God uses trials to burn off the dross in our lives and purify our faith.

If nothing was left after the purifying process, the goldsmith knew there was no real gold content. Judas Iscariot is an example of one who was tested but failed to demonstrate true faith.

2. The application

When people suffer pain, anxiety, grief, or trouble of any kind, they look for a source of comfort and relief. Most turn to friends, money, alcohol, drugs, sex, or other temporal things. But none of those brings lasting joy or relief.

In contrast, the Christian's source of joy is unchangeable and eternal. It is grounded in a hope that is "an anchor of the soul, a hope both sure and steadfast" (Heb. 6:19). If we retain that hope in the midst of trials, our faith is proved to be genuine, and our joy is multiplied.

3. The illustrations

   a) Jesus

   In the parable of the sower, Jesus said, "The one on whom seed was sown on the rocky places, this is the man who hears the word [of the kingdom], and immediately receives it with joy; yet he has no firm root in himself, but is only temporary, and when affliction or persecution arises because of the word, immediately he falls away" (Matt. 13:20-21). Persecution exposed a faith that was not genuine.

   b) Abraham

   In Genesis 22 God tested Abraham by asking him to sacrifice his son Isaac. That was a difficult test because all God's covenant promises to him were bound up in Isaac, the son of promise. But Abraham obeyed without hesitation because he believed God would keep His promises even if He had to resurrect Isaac from the dead (Heb. 11:19).

   Only divine intervention prevented Abraham from sacrificing Isaac: "The angel of the Lord called to him from heaven, and said, 'Abraham, Abraham!' And he said, 'Here I am.' And he said, 'Do not stretch out your hand against the lad, and do nothing to him; for now I know that you fear God, since you have not withheld your son, your only son, from Me'" (Gen. 22:11-12). Abraham passed the test, and his faith was confirmed (cf. James 2:21-23).

   c) Job

   Job was put to the test, and his faith eventually proved to be real. No matter what Satan did to him or what his wife and friends said, Job ultimately trusted God (Job 1:22; 2:10).

d) The Israelites

Exodus 16:4 says, "The Lord said to Moses, 'Behold, I will rain bread from heaven for you; and the people shall go out and gather a day's portion every day, that I may test them, whether or not they will walk in My instruction.'"

Moses said to the Israelites, "You shall remember all the way which the Lord your God has led you in the wilderness these forty years, that He might humble you, testing you, to know what was in your heart, whether you would keep His commandments or not" (Deut. 8:2).

e) The apostles

Acts 5:41 says the apostles were "rejoicing that they had been considered worthy to suffer shame for [Christ's] name." I'm sure their sufferings also instilled a great sense of confidence in the reality of their salvation. So often Jesus had called them men of little faith (e.g., Matt. 6:30; 8:26; 16:8). Peter denied Him openly, and all except John had forsaken Him at the cross. Yet through suffering they came to the point where they stood for Christ and did not vacillate. They passed the test.

C. The Preciousness of Proved Faith

Proved faith is a precious commodity—more precious than gold, which can pass the test of fire but is temporal and perishable. Proved faith is eternal.

The refinement of gold is an appropriate metaphor because it was the most precious of metals and the standard of all monetary transactions. But as precious and pure as gold is, proved faith is more precious by far.

Do You Welcome Trials?

If you have doubts about your faith, God may test and strengthen it by bringing trials into your life. I remember a time during my youth when I doubted my faith. God used many trials to teach me lessons that I was sometimes slow to learn. Yet experiencing those trials gave me the tremendous benefit of knowing that my faith is real.

We should welcome trials and view them as opportunities to increase our confidence and joy.

Conclusion

We have a hope that brings us joy because it is fixed on a protected inheritance and a proved faith. We should live each day in the light of that joy. It is secure in Christ—no one can take it from us (John 16:22).

Donald Grey Barnhouse told the story of a Scotsman, who "years ago . . . arrived in Liverpool where he was to embark for his journey to America. He fingered the few shillings that made up his total earthly capital, and decided that he would economize on food during the trip in order to have more money on hand when he reached New York. He went to a small store and [purchased] a supply of crackers and cheese to get him through the days at sea.

"But as the voyage progressed the sea air made him very hungry. To make matters worse the dampness in the air made his crackers soft and his cheese hard. He was almost desperate with hunger. To [top things off] he caught the fragrant whiff of food on a tray a steward was carrying to another passenger.

"The hungry man made up his mind that he would have one good, square meal, even though it might take several of his shillings. He awaited the return of the steward and asked him how much it would cost to go to the dining room and get a dinner. The steward asked the Scotsman if he had a ticket for the steamship passage. The man showed his ticket, and the steward told him that all meals were included in the price of the ticket. The poor man could have saved the money he spent on crackers and cheese; he could have gone to the dining room and eaten as much as he liked every meal time" (*Let Me Illustrate* [Old Tappan, N.J.: Revell, 1967], pp. 185-86).

Don't be a crackers-and-cheese Christian, distressed by your present circumstances and failing to experience joy when it is rightfully yours. Remember your eternal inheritance and God's purposes in the trials you face.

Focusing on the Facts

1. How does unconfessed sin affect our joy (see p. 42)?
2. What were the circumstances of those to whom Peter wrote (see pp. 42-43)?
3. Identify three companions of joy (1 Pet. 1:6-9; see pp. 43-44).
4. What is the primary difference between joy and happiness (see p. 44)?
5. What does the Greek word translated "greatly rejoice" mean (1 Pet. 1:6; see p. 44)?
6. To what does the phrase "in this" refer in 1 Peter 1:6 (see p. 45)?
7. What two historical events prove that our inheritance is protected (see pp. 45-46)?
8. Christian joy is largely the joy of _____ (see p. 47).
9. What five aspects of trouble does Peter give in 1 Peter 1:6 (see pp. 48-49)?
10. What analogy did Peter use to illustrate God's process for testing our faith (1 Pet. 1:7; see p. 49)?
11. How did God test Abraham's faith (see p. 50)?
12. According to Acts 5:41, how did the apostles respond to suffering (see p. 51)?
13. We should welcome trials and see them as opportunities to increase our _____ and _____ (see p. 52).

Pondering the Principles

1. We have seen that God uses trials and suffering to test and purify our faith. But some trials are the consequences of our sin or improper behavior. In his first epistle, Peter distinguishes be-

tween the two types of trials and gives guidelines for proper behavior so that we can avoid self-imposed trials and rejoice when
God allows trials for our testing. Read 1 Peter 1:18–3:17; 4:12-19
and answer these questions:

- What is the basis for our suffering (1 Pet. 2:19-20; 3:13-17; 4:14-
  16, 19)?
- Who is our example of suffering (1 Pet. 2:21-23)?
- How should Christian wives respond to their unbelieving
  husbands (1 Pet. 3:1-4)?
- How should we respond to those who speak against us (1 Pet.
  2:23; 3:8-12)?
- What should be our response to suffering (1 Pet. 4:12-14, 19)?

2. Unconfessed sin will quickly rob us of our joy. Psalms 32 and 51
   record David's prayers of confession and subsequent joy. Read
   those psalms and ask God to keep your heart sensitive to righteousness and ready to confess and turn away from sin.

4
The Joy of Salvation—Part 2

Outline

Introduction
A. The Pattern of Joy
B. The Prerequisite to Joy

Review
  I. A Protected Inheritance (v. 6a)
 II. A Proved Faith (vv. 6-7a)

Lesson
III. A Promised Honor (v. 7b)
   A. Its Recipients
   B. Its Elements
     1. Praise
     2. Glory
     3. Honor
       a) The definition of honor
       b) The fact of honor
   C. Its Basis
   D. Its Timing
   E. Its Assurance
IV. A Personal Fellowship (v. 8)
   A. Consisting of Love and Trust
     1. Love
       a) Defined
       b) Applied
     2. Trust
   B. Contrasted with Peter's Failure
   C. Culminating in Spiritual Growth

   D. Characterized by Joy
      1. It is inexpressible
      2. It is glorious
V. A Present Deliverance (v. 9)
   A. The Reality of Our Present Deliverance
   B. The Necessity of Our Present Deliverance

Conclusion

Introduction

A. The Pattern of Joy

Throughout Scripture those who love and obey God are characterized as people of joy. We see that especially in the book of Psalms.

1. Psalm 4:7—"Thou hast put gladness in my heart."

2. Psalm 5:11—"Let all who take refuge in Thee be glad, let them ever sing for joy."

3. Psalm 9:2—"I will be glad and exult [rejoice] in Thee; I will sing praise to Thy name, O Most High."

4. Psalm 32:11—"Be glad in the Lord and rejoice you righteous ones, and shout for joy all you who are upright in heart."

5. Psalm 37:4—"Delight yourself in the Lord."

6. Psalm 43:3-5—"O send out Thy light and Thy truth, let them lead me; let them bring me to Thy holy hill, and to Thy dwelling places. Then I will go to the altar of God, to God my exceeding joy; and upon the lyre I shall praise Thee, O God, my God. Why are you in despair, O my soul? And why are you disturbed within me? Hope in God, for I shall again praise Him, the help of my countenance, and my God."

B. The Prerequisite to Joy

Christians need never despair because our hope is in God, who has given us a supernatural joy that transcends our circumstances. Although it is His will that we reflect His joy in every area of our lives (Phil. 3:1; 4:4), sometimes we aren't joyful and need to be reminded to focus on our spiritual resources and eternal inheritance rather than on our circumstances.

Review

First Peter 1:5-9 mentions five things in which we should rejoice: a protected inheritance, a proved faith, a promised honor, a personal fellowship, and a present deliverance.

I. A PROTECTED INHERITANCE (v. 6a; see pp. 44-47)

"In this you greatly rejoice."

Hebrews 10:32-33 says, "Remember the former days, when, after being enlightened, you endured a great conflict of sufferings, partly, by being made a public spectacle through reproaches and tribulations, and partly by becoming sharers with those who were so treated. For you showed sympathy to the prisoners, and accepted joyfully the seizure of your property, knowing that you have for yourselves a better possession and an abiding one."

Those Christians joyfully accepted the seizure of their earthly property because they knew their heavenly inheritance was abiding and could never be seized or confiscated. That should be our perspective as well.

II. A PROVED FAITH (vv. 6-7a; see pp. 47-52)

"In this you greatly rejoice, even though now for a little while, if necessary, you have been distressed by various trials, that the proof of your faith, being more precious than gold which is perishable, even though tested by fire."

The great preacher Charles H. Spurgeon observed that the steps by which we ascend to the place of joy are usually moist with tears. Amid the ashes of our pain lie the sparks of our joy ready to flame up when breathed on by the Holy Spirit (cf. Spurgeon's sermons on 1 Pet. 1:6 and 7: *The Treasury of the Bible: New Testament*, vol. 4 [London: Marshall, Morgan and Scott, 1963], pp. 346-54). We can experience joy in the midst of pain if we understand that God uses pain to reveal the genuineness of our faith. The result is a proved faith that is more precious than gold.

Lesson

III. A PROMISED HONOR (v. 7b)

"May be found to result in praise and glory and honor at the revelation of Jesus Christ."

A. Its Recipients

The Greek word translated "that" in verse 7 ("that the proof of your faith") indicates the ultimate purpose for which faith is tested. In addition to the joy of knowing that our faith is real, proved faith produces the joy of anticipated reward—the praise, glory, and honor we will receive when Jesus comes. At that point our proved faith will become an honored faith.

B. Its Elements

1. Praise

The wonderful reality that we receive praise from the Lord is reflected throughout Scripture.

a) 1 Peter 2:20—"What credit is there if, when you sin and are harshly treated, you endure it with patience? But if when you do what is right and suffer for it you patiently endure it, this finds favor with God."

The Greek word translated "favor" (*charis*) speaks of "grace, thanks, excellence. [It] is used here in the sense of that which is admirable, enhancing the esteem in which those who display it are held" (*Linguistic Key to the Greek New Testament*, p. 754).

b) Matthew 25:21, 23—In the parable of the talents, the master said to his faithful servants, "Well done, good and faithful slave; you were faithful with a few things, I will put you in charge of many things, enter into the joy of your master." That's a picture of the praise and reward believers will receive from God.

c) Romans 2:29—"He is a Jew who is one inwardly; and circumcision is that which is of the heart, by the Spirit, not by the letter; and his praise is not from men, but from God."

At the revelation of Jesus Christ (Gk., *apokalupsis*; lit., "appearing," "unveiling," or "manifestation") all believers will receive praise. I believe it will be verbal praise or commendation. We will hear, "Well done, good and faithful slave" (Matt. 25:21).

2. Glory

To receive glory from God is to be made like Christ.

a) John 1:14—"The Word [Christ] became flesh, and dwelt among us, and we beheld His glory, glory as of the only begotten from the Father, full of grace and truth."

Jesus is the incarnation of God's glory, and "we know that, when He appears, we shall be like Him, because we shall see Him just as He is" (1 John 3:2).

b) Romans 2:7—Paul spoke of those who "by perseverance in doing good seek for glory and honor and immortality." As a result "glory and honor and peace" will be granted to them (v. 10).

3. Honor

a) The definition of honor

Peter probably used "honor" as a synonym for rewards, which God will give to those who faithfully serve Him.

b) The fact of honor

(1) Revelation 22:12—Jesus said, "Behold, I am coming quickly, and My reward is with Me, to render to every man according to what he has done."

(2) 1 Corinthians 3:8—"He who plants and he who waters are one; but each will receive his own reward according to his own labor."

(3) 2 John 8—"Watch yourselves, that you might not lose what we have accomplished, but that you may receive a full reward."

C. Its Basis

It is incredible that God, who alone is worthy of praise, glory, and honor, will give us all three. He will do so because we will be in the image of Jesus Christ—full possessors of His righteousness and fully endowed with the perfection of body and soul that only glorification can produce (1 John 3:2). By God's wonderful grace we will then be worthy of praise, glory, and honor.

D. Its Timing

"The revelation of Jesus Christ" (1 Pet. 1:7) includes a time also known as "the day of Christ" (e.g., Phil. 1:6), when Jesus will return to reward believers (2 Cor. 5:10). It is mentioned or alluded to throughout the New Testament (see also 1 Cor. 1:8; 5:5; 2 Cor. 1:14; Phil. 1:10).

1. 1 Peter 1:13—"Gird your minds for action, keep sober in spirit, fix your hope completely on the grace [i.e., praise, glory, and honor] to be brought to you at the revelation of Jesus Christ."

2. 1 Peter 4:13—"To the degree that you share the sufferings of Christ, keep on rejoicing; so that also at the revelation of His glory, you may rejoice with exultation."

In some sense our future reward is connected to our present faithfulness in the midst of suffering. Apparently when Christ's glory is revealed, we will be rewarded with a greater joy if we have expressed joy in this life.

3. 1 Corinthians 1:7-8—"Awaiting eagerly the revelation of our Lord Jesus Christ, who shall also confirm you to the end, blameless in the day of our Lord Jesus Christ." Paul equated "the revelation of our Lord" with "the day of our Lord Jesus Christ."

4. 2 Thessalonians 1:5-10—"This is a plain indication of God's righteous judgment so that you may be considered worthy of the kingdom of God, for which indeed you are suffering. For after all it is only just for God to repay with affliction those who afflict you, and to give relief to you who are afflicted and to us as well when the Lord Jesus shall be revealed from heaven with His mighty angels in flaming fire, dealing out retribution to those who do not know God and to those who do not obey the gospel of our Lord Jesus.

"And these will pay with the penalty of eternal destruction, away from the presence of the Lord and from the glory of His power, when He comes to be glorified in His saints on that day, and to be marveled at among all who have believed for our testimony to you was believed." Believers who have been raptured and glorified will accompany Christ and the angels when He comes to judge sinners.

5. Romans 8:18—Paul said, "I consider that the sufferings of this present time are not worthy to be compared with the glory that is to be revealed to us." Our proved faith will be gloriously rewarded at the revelation of Christ.

E. Its Assurance

Now Peter is not saying we must wait for the revelation of Christ to know if our faith is genuine. Assurance is the result of the Holy Spirit's bearing "witness with our spirit that we are children of God" (Rom. 8:16) and the proving of our faith through trials. The witness of the Spirit is the subjective (internal) affirmation of the genuineness of our faith; proved faith is its objective (external) affirmation. Peter's emphasis is the reward that awaits proved faith. We should live each day in joyful, eager anticipation of that reward.

Have You Considered Your Heavenly Reward?

When we get to heaven we will be perfect in body and spirit, and we will exercise authority and dominion with Christ Himself. The power and presence of sin will be broken forever—never again to exercise its crippling effect on our lives and relationships. We will have perfect pleasure, knowledge, comfort, love, delight, peace, and joy.

In addition we will have fellowship with God—the supreme relationship of heaven. We will see the Lord in close and intimate communion—the supreme vision of heaven. We will be loved and adored by Him—the supreme honor of heaven. We will reign and share His glory—the supreme privilege of heaven. And we will serve Him—the supreme duty of heaven. What a joyous prospect! Do you rejoice in all that God has in store for you?

In Luke 12:35-37 Jesus says, "Be dressed in readiness, and keep your lamps alight. And be like men who are waiting for their master when he returns from the wedding feast, so that they may immediately open the door to him when he comes and knocks. Blessed are those slaves whom the master shall find on the alert when he comes; truly I say to you, that he will gird himself to serve, and have them recline at table, and will come up and wait on them."

When Jesus comes for us, not only will we serve Him but He will serve us and bestow on us His praise, glory, and honor.

IV. A PERSONAL FELLOWSHIP (v. 8)

"Though you have not seen Him, you love Him, and though you do not see Him now, but believe in Him, you greatly rejoice with joy inexpressible and full of glory."

A. Consisting of Love and Trust

1. Love

    It is normal to love someone with whom you've had personal contact. But Peter was writing to Christians who, like us, had never met Jesus face to face. They had never touched Him, walked with Him, shared a meal with Him, heard His voice, felt His hands, or gazed into His eyes. Yet they loved Him.

    a) Defined

    The present active indicative form of the verb "to love" (Gk., *agapaō*) describes their constant, sustained love for Christ. *Agapaō* is the love of the will—a love of choice. They had chosen to faithfully love Him.

    b) Applied

    I believe that an intimate love relationship with Christ is the essence of true joy. In addition, it is the hallmark of a true Christian.

    (1) 1 Peter 2:7—"Unto you . . . who believe [Jesus] is precious" (KJV).

    (2) 1 Corinthians 16:22—Paul said, "If anyone does not love the Lord, let him be accursed." The Greek word translated "accursed" means "cursed" or "devoted to destruction." It is a strong statement of condemnation.

    If you doubt someone's claim to Christianity, ask him what he thinks of Jesus. If he describes an intimate and consuming love for Him, he has a transformed heart.

(3) 1 John 4:19—"We love, because He first loved us." Our love is a response to His love.

(4) Matthew 22:37—Jesus said, "You shall love the Lord your God with all your heart, and with all your soul, and with all your mind."

(5) Ephesians 6:24—Paul said, "Grace be with all those who love our Lord Jesus Christ with a love incorruptible." Anyone who doesn't love the Lord Jesus Christ cannot be a Christian.

(6) John 14:15, 21, 24—Jesus said, "If you love Me, you will keep My commandments. . . . He who has My commandments and keeps them, he it is who loves Me. . . . He who does not love Me does not keep My words." Jesus equated loving Him with obeying Him. Therefore a true believer is one who loves and obeys Christ.

2. Trust

Those who have not seen Christ yet love Him and believe in Him demonstrate the two key ingredients in any good relationship: love and trust. That is in contrast to the disciple Thomas, to whom Jesus said, "Because you have seen Me, have you believed? Blessed are they who did not see, and yet believed" (John 20:29). Love and trust establish an intimate bond with Christ that brings "joy inexpressible and full of glory" (1 Pet. 1:8).

B. Contrasted with Peter's Failure

Love and trust are so crucial to intimacy that if either are violated the relationship begins to disintegrate. Peter understood that principle from personal experience. With the exception of Judas Iscariot, Peter demonstrated the least degree of trust of any disciple, denying Christ three times (Matt. 26:69-75). And Jesus repeatedly questioned the quality of his love (John 21:15-17), at one time saying to him, "O you of little faith, why did you doubt?" (Matt. 14:31).

64

As Peter was commending his readers for loving and trusting Christ, whom they had not seen, I'm sure he was mindful of his failure to do the same thing even though he had spent three years in Christ's presence.

Even though Peter failed, the Lord graciously forgave him and restored him to ministry. And Peter learned to love and trust Christ deeply. In the same way, God's Spirit patiently teaches us to love and trust the Lord.

C. Culminating in Spiritual Growth

First Corinthians 13:7 says that love "believes all things." Love and trust are so inextricably linked that if we truly believe, we truly love and vice versa. That principle is evident in the cycle of Christian growth: God grants us faith, and by faith we accept the biblical teachings about Jesus Christ. As our knowledge of Him increases, our love and trust grow correspondingly. Consequently we desire to glorify Him by serving Him wholeheartedly, talking about Him, reading about Him, sharing fellowship with Him, getting to know Him better, and becoming increasingly like Him.

Seventeenth-century Anglican archbishop Robert Leighton said, "Believe, and you shall love; believe much, and you shall love much; labour for strong and deep persuasions of the glorious things which are spoken of Christ, and this will command love. Certainly, did men indeed believe his worth, they would accordingly love him; for the reasonable creature cannot but affect that most which it firmly believes to be the worthiest of affection. Oh! this mischievous unbelief is that which makes the heart cold and dead towards God. Seek then to believe Christ's excellency in himself, and his love to us, and our interest in him, and this will kindle such a fire in the heart, as will make it ascend in a sacrifice of love to him" (*Commentary on First Peter* [Grand Rapids: Kregel, 1972 reprint], p. 55).

His words reiterate that love and trust are at the heart of our relationship to Christ. Do you enjoy that kind of relationship? If so, you know what great joy it brings—the joy of meditating on Christ, communing with Him in prayer, knowing your faith is secure in Him, and expressing love to One who is so worthy.

D. Characterized by Joy

Our Lord said, "It is more blessed to give than to receive" (Acts 20:36). That's especially true when it comes to love and the joy it brings.

1. It is inexpressible

Peter spoke of "joy inexpressible and full of glory" (1 Pet. 1:8). The Greek word translated "inexpressible" (*anekla-lētos*) means "unspeakable, inexpressible, ineffable. The word contains the sense of a divine mystery exceeding the powers of speech and thought" (*Linguistic Key to the Greek New Testament*, p. 745).

Even on a human level it is difficult to communicate the joy of loving others—as evidenced by the thousands of love songs that attempt to do so. But beyond that is the inexpressible joy that comes from loving Christ.

2. It is glorious

Our joy is also "full of glory" (v. 8). It is infused and energized with divine glory. It isn't a human joy but a supernatural endowment—a fruit of the Spirit (Gal. 5:22), just as our love for Christ also is a gift (cf. 1 John 4:19). Our joy is a heavenly joy because our love is a heavenly love.

V. A PRESENT DELIVERANCE (v. 9)

"Obtaining as the outcome of your faith the salvation of your souls."

A. The Reality of Our Present Deliverance

The Greek word translated "obtaining" (*komizō*) is here used in its present middle participle form. A literal translation is, "Presently receiving for yourselves." It means, "'to obtain something that is due to a person.' In this case, [it] signifies that through the work of Christ the believer obtains salvation. Already in this life the Christian claims for himself the salvation Christ provides (see 1 Cor. 1:18)" (Simon J. Kistemaker, *New Testament Commentary: 1 Peter* [Grand Rapids: Baker, 1987], pp. 50-51).

Our joy is linked to the present, ongoing salvation of our souls. The phrase "outcome of your faith" refers to the logical result or logical end of faith. The Greek word translated "souls" speaks of the whole person. "This is not a special part of man's structure but is man as a whole; it is a Jewish rather than a [Greek] or modern usage of the word" (*Linguistic Key to the Greek New Testament*, p. 746). Salvation affects your entire life. Verse 9 could be translated: "You rejoice because you have and continue to hold onto the logical result of your proved faith—your ongoing deliverance from sin."

B. The Necessity of Our Present Deliverance

We need to be constantly delivered from sin, guilt, condemnation, wrath, ignorance, distress, confusion, hopelessness, and everything else that is part of man's fallen, defiled nature. We rejoice in knowing we are no longer slaves to sin's power, passions, and pleasures. Christ has given us new life and made us new creatures (2 Cor. 5:17).

Our present salvation rescues us from the sordid, damning, and scarring effects of sin and causes us to long for Christ. It calls us to no longer drink from the mud puddle of sin but to partake of the crystal streams of the fountain of eternal life. Although we live in a sinful world and are exposed to various trials and temptations, sin no longer has dominion over us, and we can rejoice in the assurance that God will never test us beyond what we are able to endure (1 Cor. 10:13).

Conclusion

There is no reason for us ever to lose our joy, because we can look to our protected inheritance, proved faith, promised honor, and present deliverance. We must learn to tap those resources. Jesus said, "These things I have spoken to you, that My joy may be in you, and that your joy may be full" (John 15:11). He wants every Christian to be full of joy.

The hymn titled "Jesus, I Am Resting," written by Jean Sophia Pigott during the last century, contains these lovely words:

Jesus, I am resting
Resting in the joy of what Thou art;
I am finding out the greatness
Of Thy loving heart.

Such joy was also expressed by Bernard of Clairvaux, the twelfth-century French monk, in the familiar hymn "Jesus, Thou Joy of Loving Hearts." Those hymns reflect the exuberance of Christians throughout the centuries and in varying circumstances who have experienced the joy of their spiritual resources. God wants us to live that way, too. I trust you will know the full measure of joy that loving Christ can bring.

Focusing on the Facts

1. What enabled the Christians in Hebrews 10:32-33 to endure severe persecution (see p. 57)?
2. List three ingredients of our promised honor (1 Pet. 1:7; see pp. 58-59).
3. What words of praise did the faithful slaves in Matthew 25 receive from their master (see p. 59)?
4. What does it mean to receive glory from God (see p. 59)?
5. What is a synonym for "honor" as used in 1 Peter 1:7 (see p. 60)?
6. According to 2 Thessalonians 1:6-9, what will happen to unbelievers when Christ returns to earth (see p. 61)?
7. What kind of love did the recipients of 1 Peter have for Jesus (1 Pet. 1:8; see p. 63)?
8. _____ and _____ are so crucial to intimacy that if either is violated, the relationship begins to disintegrate (see p. 64).
9. How does 1 Peter 1:8 contrast with Peter's own experience (Matt. 26:69-75; see pp. 64-65)?
10. Define "inexpressible" as used in 1 Peter 1:8 (see p. 66).
11. What did Peter mean by "obtaining as the outcome of your faith the salvation of your souls" (1 Pet. 1:9; see pp. 66-67)?

Pondering the Principles

1. It is wonderful to consider that someday Jesus will bestow honor upon us (1 Pet. 1:7). In the meantime we are commanded to

honor one another by being devoted to each another in brotherly love and giving preference to one another (Rom. 12:10). Jesus illustrated such an attitude by washing His disciples' feet (John 13:3-6). Paul illustrated it by setting aside some of his apostolic rights for the sake of winning more people to Christ (1 Cor. 9:1-19). How might you show honor and preference to others today?

2. A day is coming when Christ Himself will evaluate everything we have done. Paul said, "We must all appear before the judgment seat of Christ, that each one may be recompensed for his deeds in the body, according to what he has done, whether good or bad [lit. "valuable" or "worthless"]" (2 Cor. 5:10). Although that day will be a time of rewards, some of our works might be revealed as worthless (1 Cor. 3:12-14). That should motivate us to turn from worthless pursuits and to live righteously with a view toward pleasing the Lord. In Philippians 1:9-11 Paul gives us helpful instructions on how to do that. Read that passage with the prayer that God will help you to pursue the things that are excellent and of highest value to Him.

5
The Greatness of Our Salvation

Outline

Introduction
A. Peter's Purpose
B. Peter's Perspective

Lesson
I. The Prophets' Study (vv. 10-11a)
   A. The Goals of Their Study
      1. To understand salvation
      2. To understand the Messiah
   B. The Subject of Their Study
      1. The nature of God's grace
      2. The extent of God's grace
         a) To Israel
         b) To Nineveh
         c) To all nations
   C. The Findings of Their Study
      1. With regard to the Messiah
         a) He would suffer
         b) He would triumph
         c) He would bring about salvation
      2. With regard to us
   D. Their Method of Study
   E. The Time of Their Study
II. The Holy Spirit's Inspiration (vv. 11b-12a)
   A. The Fact of Inspiration (v. 11b)
   B. The Process of Inspiration (v. 11c)
   C. The Focus of Inspiration (v. 11d)
      1. The sufferings of Christ
      2. The glory of Christ

    D. The Fulfillment of Inspiration (v. 12*a*)
III. The Apostles' Proclamation (v. 12*b*)
    A. The Message of the Preachers
    B. The Identity of the Preachers
    C. The Commitment of the Preachers
IV. The Angels' Interest (v. 12*b*)
    A. The Intensity of Their Interest in Salvation
    B. The Reasons for Their Interest in Salvation
        1. They can't experience it
        2. They played a role in it
        3. They want to glorify God for it

Conclusion

Introduction

A. Peter's Purpose

First Peter 1:1-12 calls us to praise God for our eternal inheritance and the greatness of our salvation. Verses 3-4 state we have been "born again to a living hope through the resurrection of Jesus Christ from the dead, to obtain an inheritance which is imperishable and undefiled and will not fade away, reserved in heaven for [us]." No matter what trials God may use to test and strengthen our faith, we can "rejoice with joy inexpressible and full of glory" (v. 8) because proved faith affirms the reality of our salvation.

B. Peter's Perspective

In verses 10-12 Peter describes the greatness of salvation in an unusual way. Rather than presenting it from man's perspective, he presented it from the perspectives of the Old Testament prophets, the Holy Spirit, the New Testament apostles, and the angels. The prophets studied it, the Spirit inspired it, the apostles preached it, and the angels long to understand it.

I. THE PROPHETS' STUDY (vv. 10-11*a*)

"As to this salvation, the prophets who prophesied of the grace that would come to you made careful search and inquiry, seeking to know what person or time."

The prophets studied their own writings to learn all they could about the salvation God was proclaiming through them. "Prophets" is a general reference to all Old Testament prophets, from Moses to Malachi.

A. The Goals of Their Study

1. To understand salvation

   It is appropriate that the prophets chose salvation from among all the themes they might have studied. God's wondrous grace to sinners is the greatest theme in the universe, and it was their passion to understand it.

   Although the prophets were saved by faith just as we are, their understanding of salvation was limited because they never saw it accomplished through the life, death, and resurrection of Jesus Christ.

2. To understand the Messiah

   In addition, they longed to understand God's plan to extend salvation beyond Israel to all the nations of the earth through the Messiah.

B. The Subject of Their Study

The prophets intently studied the saving grace of God that was to come at a future time.

1. The nature of God's grace

   The Greek word translated "grace" speaks of God's unearned favor and blessing toward sinners. It is broader in scope than the word *salvation* because *grace* encompasses both the act of salvation and the motives behind it.

2. The extent of God's grace

"The grace that would come" (v. 10) does not mean that grace was absent from the Old Testament. Many people wrongly assume that the Old Testament is all law and no grace. That's not true. God is by nature gracious (1 Pet. 5:10), and His nature never changes (James 1:17). We see many examples of His grace in the Old Testament.

a) To Israel

(1) Genesis 43:29—"As [Joseph] lifted his eyes and saw his brother Benjamin . . . he said . . . 'May God be gracious to you.'" Even in the first book of the Bible the patriarchs were aware of God's grace.

(2) Exodus 22:26-27—God said to Israel, "If you ever take your neighbor's cloak as a pledge, you are to return it to him before the sun sets, for that is his only covering; it is his cloak for his body. What else shall he sleep in? And it shall come about that when he cries out to Me, I will hear him, for I am gracious."

(3) Exodus 33:19—God said to Moses, "I Myself will make all My goodness pass before you, and will proclaim the name of the Lord before you; and I will be gracious to whom I will be gracious, and will show compassion on whom I will show compassion."

(4) The Psalms—The book of Psalms is replete with statements about the grace of God. The fact that He didn't instantly consume all sinners is one indication of His grace.

b) To Nineveh

The prophet Jonah made this admission: "I fled to Tarshish, for I knew that Thou art a gracious and compassionate God" (Jonah 4:2). Jonah ran from God because he feared that if he preached to the Ninevites, they would repent and God would show mercy to them. He was so prejudiced he couldn't stand the thought of Gentiles being saved.

c) To all nations

(1) Isaiah 45:20-24—"Gather yourselves and come; draw near together, you fugitives of the nations; they have no knowledge, who carry about their wooden idol, and pray to a god who cannot save. Declare and set forth your case; indeed, let them consult together. Who has announced this from of old? Who has long since declared it? Is it not I, the Lord? And there is no other God beside Me, a righteous God and a Savior" (vv. 20-21). God was announcing that He is a Savior to all nations.

The context continues, "There is none except Me. Turn to Me, and be saved, all the ends of the earth; for I am God and there is no other. I have sworn by Myself, the word has gone forth from My mouth in righteousness and will not turn back, that to Me every knee will bow, every tongue will swear allegiance. They will say of Me, 'Only in the Lord are righteousness and strength.' Men will come to Him" (vv. 21-24).

(2) Isaiah 55:1-5—"Ho! Every one who thirsts, come to the waters. And you who have no money come, buy and eat. Come, buy wine and milk without money and without cost. Why do you spend money for what is not bread [follow false gods], and your wages for what does not satisfy?

"Listen carefully to Me, and eat what is good, and delight yourself in abundance. Incline your ear and come to Me. Listen, that you may live; and I will make an everlasting covenant with you, according to the faithful mercies shown to David.

"Behold, I have made him a witness to the [nations], a leader and commander for the peoples. Behold, you will call a nation you do not know, and a nation which knows you not will run to you, because of the Lord your God, even the Holy One of Israel." That is an invitation to all nations to partake of salvation.

C. The Findings of Their Study

1. With regard to the Messiah

Their prophecies contained several facts about Messiah.

a) He would suffer

Psalm 22 details His crucifixion and Isaiah 53 details His suffering.

b) He would triumph

(1) Psalm 16:10—David said, "Thou wilt not abandon my soul to Sheol; neither wilt Thou allow Thy Holy One to undergo decay" (cf. Acts 13:35).

(2) Psalm 2:6, 9—The Lord said, "I have installed My King upon Zion, My holy mountain. . . . Ask of Me, and I will surely give the nations as Thine inheritance, and the very ends of the earth as Thy possession. Thou shalt break them with a rod of iron."

(3) Isaiah 9:6—"A child will be born to us, a son will be given to us; and the government will rest on His shoulders; and His name will be called Wonderful Counselor, Mighty God."

c) He would bring about salvation

Luke 4:16-21 says, "[Jesus] came to Nazareth, where He had been brought up; and as was His custom, He entered the synagogue on the Sabbath, and stood up to read. And the book of the prophet Isaiah was handed to Him.

"And He opened the book, and found the place where it was written, 'The Spirit of the Lord is upon Me, because He anointed Me to preach the gospel to the poor. He has sent Me to proclaim release to the captive, and recovery of sight to the blind, to set free those who are downtrodden, to proclaim the favorable year of the Lord' [Isa. 61:1-2].

"And He closed the book, and gave it back to the attendant, and sat down; and the eyes of all in the synagogue were fixed upon Him. And He began to say to them, 'Today this Scripture has been fulfilled in your hearing.'" There Jesus was discussing salvation through the Messiah in a Jewish context.

The apostle Paul quoted from a number of Old Testament prophecies regarding Gentile salvation.

(1) Romans 9:25-26—"[God] says also in Hosea, 'I will call those who were not My people, "My people," and her who was not beloved, "Beloved."' 'And it shall be that in the place where it was said to them, "You are not My people," there they shall be called sons of the living God'" (cf. Hos. 1:10; 2:23).

(2) Romans 9:33; 10:11—"I lay in Zion a stone of stumbling and a rock of offense, and he who believes in Him will not be disappointed" (cf. Isa. 28:16).

(3) Romans 10:13—"Whoever will call upon the name of the Lord will be saved" (cf. Joel 2:32).

(4) Romans 10:20-21—God said, "'I was found by those who sought Me not, I became manifest to those who did not ask for Me.' But as for Israel He says, 'All the day long I have stretched out My hands to a disobedient and obstinate people'" (cf. Isa. 65:1-2).

(5) Romans 15:9—"The Gentiles [will] glorify God for His mercy; as it is written, 'Therefore I will give praise to Thee among the Gentiles, and I will sing to Thy name'" (cf. Ps. 18:49).

(6) Romans 15:10—"Rejoice, O Gentiles, with His people" (cf. Deut. 32:43).

(7) Romans 15:12—"There shall come the root of Jesse, and He who arises to rule over the Gentiles, in Him shall the Gentiles hope" (cf. Isa. 11:1).

(8) Romans 15:21—"They who had no news of Him shall see, and they who have not heard shall understand" (cf. Isa. 52:15).

Paul clearly indicated that the Old Testament messianic prophecies were fulfilled in Jesus Christ.

2. With regard to us

First Peter 1:10 says, "The prophets . . . prophesied of the grace that would come *to you*" (emphasis added). That applies not only to Peter's audience but also to everyone who believes in Jesus Christ.

D. Their Method of Study

The prophets wrote long before the birth of Christ, the existence of the church, the unity of Jewish and Gentile believers in Christ, or the writings of the apostles. Therefore their knowledge of a future salvation through the Messiah was limited to what they could learn from their own writings and the writings of their fellow prophets. Those writings were the focus of their "careful search and inquiry" (1 Pet. 1:10).

The Greek words translated "search" (*exetazō*) and "inquiry" (*exeraunaō*) do not have distinct meanings. Both are in a compound form, which intensifies their meaning. They are used together to emphasize the thoroughness of the prophets' study.

Is Your Salvation Precious to You?

Salvation was a precious theme to the Old Testament prophets. They longed to understand it and studied hard to discover the richness of its implications. How much more should we who have experienced new life in Christ praise God for our salvation and look to it as our source of joy in times of suffering?

We have seen that the Old Testament prophets had an incomplete understanding of salvation because they preceded the coming of Christ. In Matthew 13:17 Jesus says to His disciples, "Truly I say to you, that many prophets and righteous men desired to see what you see, and did not see it; and to hear what you hear, and did not hear it." Although their information about the Messiah was limited, their passionate, driving compulsion to understand the greatness of salvation prompted them to thoroughly study their own writings.

E. The Time of Their Study

Some have suggested that Peter, in saying the prophets were "seeking to know what person or time" (v. 11) related to their prophecies, was referring to the attitude of the prophets before they received any prophecies. These people assert that the prophets' intense desire to understand salvation prompted God to give them prophecies about the Messiah.

I disagree with that view because, prior to God's revelation about God's future grace through the Messiah, the prophets would not have known that such a grace existed and would have had nothing to search and inquire into. Furthermore, God sovereignly chose the recipients of His revelation. He didn't give it on the basis of someone's request or curiosity.

Additionally, verse 11 says the prophets were specifically interested in two aspects of redemptive history. They already had enough revelation to arouse their interest; now they wanted to understand what had already been revealed. They wanted to know who the Messiah would be and when He would come.

The Greek word translated "seeking" (*eraunaō*) literally means "searching." Like many Jewish people today, they were searching for their Savior and the time (Gk., *kairos*, "season," "era," or "epoch") when He would appear.

II. THE HOLY SPIRIT'S INSPIRATION (vv. 11b-12a)

A. The Fact of Inspiration (v. 11b)

"The Spirit of Christ."

Biblical revelation was given by divine inspiration as God spoke to and through the prophets by His Spirit. "Spirit of Christ" refers to the Holy Spirit and shows that Christ existed before He came to earth in human form.

B. The Process of Inspiration (v. 11c)

"Within them was indicating."

The Spirit resided within the writers of the Old Testament. Second Peter 1:20-21 says, "No prophecy of Scripture is a matter of one's own interpretation, for no prophecy was ever made by an act of human will, but men moved by the Holy Spirit spoke from God." The Greek word translated "moved" means "carried along." It was a nautical term describing the wind as it moved a ship through the water. The Holy Spirit moved the writers of Scripture to produce God's Word.

The Greek word translated "indicating" in 1 Peter 1:11 (*promarturomai*) literally means "to witness" or "testify beforehand." The Spirit of Christ within the prophets testified of a future salvation. The written record of that testimony is the inspired Word of God (2 Tim. 3:16).

Inspiration also extended to the New Testament apostles, who "preached the gospel . . . by the Holy Spirit sent from heaven" (1 Pet. 1:12).

C. The Focus of Inspiration (v. 11d)

"As He predicted the sufferings of Christ and the glories to follow."

Inspiration covers the breadth of Scripture, but here Peter refers specifically to that which was written about Christ's suffering and glorification.

1. The sufferings of Christ

Many Old Testament passages tell of the Messiah's sufferings: Psalm 22:1-18; 69:1-21; Isaiah 52:13–53:12; Daniel 9:26; Zechariah 12:10; 13:7. It was only by the Spirit's inspiration that the prophets knew what would happen to Him.

2. The glory of Christ

"The glories to follow" refers to Christ's resurrection, ascension, enthronement, and kingly rule (Isa. 9:6; Dan. 2:44; 7:13-14; Zech. 2:10-13; 14:3-5).

The sufferings and glories of Christ are the major themes of Old Testament prophecy. Revelation 19:10 says, "The testimony of Jesus . . . is the spirit of prophecy." All prophecy directly or indirectly testifies of Christ. Jesus said to the disciples on the road to Emmaus, "O foolish men and slow of heart to believe in all that the prophets have spoken! Was it not necessary for the Christ to suffer these things and to enter into His glory?" (Luke 24:25-26).

D. The Fulfillment of Inspiration (v. 12a)

"It was revealed to them that they were not serving themselves, but you."

The Holy Spirit revealed to the prophets that their prophecies about the Messiah were not for their generation but for a future time. The prophet Balaam said, "I see him, but not now; I behold him, but not near; a star shall come forth from Jacob, and a scepter shall rise from Israel" (Num. 24:17). As early as the Pentateuch, God's Spirit testified about the coming of the Messiah.

Hebrews 11:13 says, "All [the Old Testament patriarchs] died in faith, without receiving the promises, but having seen them and having welcomed them from a distance." They could see the fulfillment of God's promises only from a distance. "Having gained approval through their faith, [they] did not receive what was promised, because God had provided something better for us, so that apart from us they should not be made perfect" (vv. 39-40).

Old Testament prophecies were not meaningless to the prophets. They had immense value. Yet the fulfillment of those prophecies was not for their generation but for the time when both Jewish and Gentile salvation would be accomplished through the Messiah.

III. THE APOSTLES' PROCLAMATION (v. 12b)

"In these things which now have been announced to you through those who preached the gospel to you by the Holy Spirit sent from heaven."

A. The Message of the Preachers

"These things" refers to all the Old Testament prophecies regarding through whom salvation would come and when it would come. That was the message of the New Testament preachers, who preached Jesus as the Christ (or Messiah) and "now" as "the day of salvation" (2 Cor. 6:2).

B. The Identity of the Preachers

"Those who preached the gospel" were men such as Paul, John, Barnabas, Philip, and Luke. They could all be considered apostles in a sense—not because they had all been among the original twelve but because they preached the apostolic message of the death and resurrection of Christ (cf. Acts 14:14; Rom. 16:7).

Paul said, "I determined to know nothing among you except Jesus Christ, and Him crucified" (1 Cor. 2:2); "I am not ashamed of the gospel, for it is the power of God for salvation to everyone who believes, to the Jew first and also to the [Gentile]" (Rom. 1:16); and "the word of the cross is to those who are perishing foolishness, but to us who are being saved it is the power of God" (1 Cor. 1:18). That is typical New Testament apostolic preaching.

C. The Commitment of the Preachers

The greatness of our salvation is such a precious, compelling theme that the apostles and their followers were willing to die if necessary to proclaim it—and many of them did.

IV. THE ANGELS' INTEREST (v. 12b)

"Things into which angels long to look."

When I was a child, I often thought about how great it would be to be an angel and fly around, doing good, and being in the presence of God. Imagine what it would be like to perceive the spiritual dimension in which they live and witness battles between holy angels and demonic forces. Such things are mysterious to us, yet our salvation is as much a mystery to the angels as their activities are to us.

A. The Intensity of Their Interest in Salvation

The Greek word translated "long" (*epithumeō*) means a strong, unfulfilled desire or overpowering impulse. In its negative sense it is often translated "lust." In this context it means that the angels have a strong, unsatisfied impulse to understand the details of our salvation.

The Greek word translated "look" literally means "to stretch forward your head," or "to bend down." In John 20:5 it describes Peter and John's peering into the empty tomb after Christ's resurrection.

B. The Reasons for Their Interest in Salvation

1. They can't experience it

   Holy angels have no need of salvation, and fallen angels cannot be saved. I believe Peter was referring to the holy angels' desire to understand salvation, but it is also possible that some fallen angels want to understand it in hopes of receiving it. However, that will not happen.

2. They played a role in it

   The holy angels announced Christ's birth, ministered to Him after His temptation, announced His resurrection and ascension, and are now doing His bidding on behalf of the saints.

   On the other hand, the fallen angels did everything they could to prevent salvation. They attacked our Lord during His temptation, besieged Him throughout His life, and tried to kill Him and prevent His resurrection. They still persist in assaulting His work and His people.

3. They want to glorify God for it

   Holy angels exist to glorify God, and the more they see His grace on display, the more they can glorify Him. So their interest in salvation goes beyond mere curiosity.

   a) Luke 15:7—Jesus said, "There will be more joy in heaven over one sinner who repents, than over ninety-nine righteous persons who need no repentance." The angels rejoice and praise God every time someone is saved.

   b) 1 Corinthians 4:9—Paul said, "God has exhibited us apostles last of all, as men condemned to death; because we have become a spectacle to the world, both to angels and to men." The angels observed Paul as God's power worked through him and his associates.

   c) Ephesians 3:10—"The manifold wisdom of God [is] now . . . made known through the church to the rulers and authorities in the heavenly places." God's grace is on display in the church.

d) Revelation 5:8-12—"When [Christ, the Lamb of God] had taken the book [the title deed to the earth], the four living creatures [angels] and the twenty-four elders [representing the saints] fell down before the Lamb, having each one a harp, and golden bowls full of incense, which are the prayers of the saints.

"And they sang a new song, saying, 'Worthy art Thou to take the book, and to break its seals; for Thou wast slain, and didst purchase for God with Thy blood men from every tribe and tongue and people and nation.' . . . And I [John] looked, and I heard the voice of many angels around the throne and the living creatures and the elders; and the number of them was myriads of myriads, and thousands of thousands, saying with a loud voice, 'Worthy is the Lamb that was slain to receive power and riches and wisdom and might and honor and glory and blessing.'"

Although angels are not recipients of salvation, they will join in singing the redemption song. As they observe and understand it, they glorify God all the more.

Conclusion

The theme of salvation was precious to the Old Testament prophets, the Holy Spirit, the New Testament apostles, and the angels. Is it precious to you? Or have you allowed sin and circumstances to rob you of your first love? When that happened to the Ephesian church, the Lord said, "Remember . . . from where you have fallen, and repent and do the deeds you did at first" (Rev. 2:5).

If you have lost sight of the preciousness and joy of your salvation, the solution is to repent and begin to live the way you did when you were saved—when you had an exhilarating love for God, a zealous testimony for Christ, a deep hunger for His Word, and a sincere desire for Christian fellowship and prayer. Those are reliable indicators that we love our Savior and appreciate our great salvation.

Focusing on the Facts

1. What were two goals of the prophets' study (1 Pet. 1:10-11; see p. 73)?
2. What does the Greek word translated "grace" mean (see pp. 73-74)?
3. Was God's grace evident in the Old Testament? Explain (see pp. 74-76).
4. Why did the prophet Jonah flee to Tarshish (Jonah 4:2; see p. 75)?
5. List three things that the Old Testament prophets knew about the Messiah (see pp. 76-78).
6. What do "search" and "inquiry" (1 Pet. 1:10) tell us about the prophet's study (see pp. 78-79)?
7. Why is it incorrect to say 1 Peter 1:10 teaches that the intense desire of the Old Testament prophets to understand salvation prompted God to grant them revelation (see pp. 79-80)?
8. To whom does "the Spirit of Christ" refer in 1 Peter 1:11 (see p. 80)?
9. Define "moved" as used in 2 Peter 1:21 (see p. 80).
10. How does 1 Peter 1:11 affirm the inspiration of the apostles (see pp. 80-81)?
11. What did Peter mean by "the glories to follow" (1 Pet. 1:11; see p. 81)?
12. Who are the preachers referred to in 1 Peter 1:12 (see pp. 82-83)?
13. Define "long" as used in 1 Peter 1:12 in reference to the angels (see p. 83).
14. List three reasons that angels desire to understand salvation (see p. 84).
15. What does Revelation 5 show us about the role of angels in relation to salvation (see p. 85)?

Pondering the Principles

1. The intense desire of the prophets to understand salvation compelled them to study their own writings diligently. That's a tre-

mendous example to us because even though we are recipients of that salvation, there is still much for us to learn from studying God's Word. Let the excitement of the prophets motivate you to "long for the pure milk of the word, that by it you may grow in respect to salvation" (1 Pet. 2:2).

2. David said, "The Lord is compassionate and gracious, slow to anger and abounding in lovingkindness" (Ps. 103:8). He is worthy of all our praise for the great salvation He has given to us. Read Psalm 103, noting all the things for which we can praise God. Then spend time in prayer, thanking Him for each one.

3. Our salvation is a wonderful and joyous thing—perhaps exceeded only by the joy of leading others to Christ. Jesus said, "There will be . . . joy in heaven over one sinner who repents" (Luke 15:7). We must never be content to keep our salvation to ourselves but must tell others about Christ as often as we can so that they may experience the joy of salvation. Look for opportunities to do that today!

Scripture Index

Genesis
14:20   17
17:8   11
22:11-12   50
24:27   17
43:29   74

Exodus
3:8   34
16:4   51
18:10   17
22:26-27   74
33:19   74
34:6   27

Numbers
21:5-9   30-31
24:17   82

Deuteronomy
8:2   51
15:4   11
19:10   11
32:6   17
32:43   78

Joshua
13:32-33   14

Job
1:22   51
2:10   51

Psalms
2:6   76
2:9   76
4:7   56
5:11   56
9:2   56

16:5   15
16:10   76
18:49   78
22:1-18   81
32:11   56
37:4   56
43:3-5   56
51:12   43
73:23-26   15
108:4   27

Isaiah
9:6   76, 81
11:1   78
28:16   77
45:20-24   75
52:13–53:12   81
52:15   78
55:1-5   75-76
61:1-2   77
65:1-2   78

Jeremiah
13:23   28
32:27   32

Lamentations
3:22-23   27
3:24   15

Daniel
2:44   81
6:19-23   37
7:13-14   81
9:26   81

Hosea
1:10   77
2:23   77

Joel
2:32   77

Micah
7:18   27

Zechariah
2:10-13   81
12:10   81
13:7   81
14:3-5   81

Matthew
5:12   44
6:19-20   34-36
6:30   51
6:33   12
8:26   51
11:27   18
13:17   79
13:20-21   50
14:31   64
16:8   51
21:31   30
22:37   64
25:21   59
25:23   59
25:34   9
25:41-46   29
26:69-75   64

Mark
10:47   26
15:34   17

Luke
4:16-21   77
12:35-37   62
15:7   84
24:25-26   81

John
1:13   31
1:14   59

3:3   29
3:5   31
3:14-16   30
4:21-23   17
5:17   18
8:42   29
10:30   18
10:31-33   18
11:25   33
11:43-44   33
14:3   45
14:9   18
14:15   64
14:19   33
14:21   64
14:24   64
15:11   67
16:16   45
16:20-22   45
16:22   52
17:1   18
17:5   18
17:21-23   19
20:5   83
20:29   64
21:15-17   64

Acts
5:41   51
13:35   76
14:14   82
20:36   66
26:18   10

Romans
1:16   83
2:7   59
2:10   59
2:29   59
5:2   46
8:9   46
8:16   11, 62
8:17   11, 15, 28
8:18   61

8:20-23	34	Ephesians		
8:28	32	1:3	18	
8:31	37	1:10-18	10	
8:33	37	1:12-14	46	
9:15	27	1:14	15	
9:25-26	77	1:17	18	
9:33	77	2:1	28	
10:9	46	2:3	28-29	
10:11	77	2:4-5	25	
10:13	77	2:8	13	
10:20-21	78	2:8-9	37	
12:12	46	2:12	28	
13:11	13-14	3:10	84-85	
15:9	78	6:24	64	
15:10	78			
15:12	78	Philippians		
15:21	78	1:6	14, 37, 60	
16:7	82	1:10	60	
		1:21	32	
1 Corinthians		1:29	37	
1:7-8	61	3:1	57	
1:8	60	3:8-9	35	
1:18	66, 83	4:4	57	
2:2	83			
2:9	12, 16	Colossians		
3:8	60	1:12	10	
4:9	84	3:2	12	
5:5	60			
6:17	19	1 Thessalonians		
10:13	67	1:9-10	13	
13:7	65			
15:17	33	2 Thessalonians		
15:19	32	1:5-10	61	
16:22	63-64			
		2 Timothy		
2 Corinthians		3:16	80	
1:3	19, 27			
1:14	60	Titus		
5:10	60	3:5	25, 31	
5:17	28, 31, 67			
6:2	82	Hebrews		
		1:14	14	
Galatians		6:19	50	
5:22	46, 66	9:15	10	

9:28	14	2:9	8, 14
10:32-33	57	2:12	42
11:13	82	2:19-21	42
11:19	50	2:20	58-59
11:39-40	82	2:21-23	8
		3:9	42
James		3:14-17	43
1:2	42	4:1	43
1:17	74	4:10	48
1:18	31	4:12-14	43
2:21-23	50	4:13	61
		4:16	43
1 Peter		5:10	43, 48, 74
1:1	9		
1:1-12	72	2 Peter	
1:2	20	3:13	32
1:3	9-20, 25-33		
1:3-4	72	1 John	
1:3-5	8-9, 16, 24-25, 45	1:9	13
1:4	10-11, 24, 33-36	2:15	12
1:5	12-13, 36-38	3:2	11, 15, 59-60
1:5-9	57	4:19	64, 66
1:6	44-49, 57		
1:6-7	57	2 John	
1:6-9	43-44	3	19
1:6-10	42	8	60
1:7	49-53, 58-62		
1:8	63-66, 72	Jude	
1:9	66-67	24	37
1:10-11	73-80		
1:10-12	72	Revelation	
1:11	80-81	2:5	85
1:12	81-86	3:21	19
1:13	60	5:8-12	85
1:20-21	80	20:2	31
1:23	13, 29, 31	21:27	36
1:25	29	22:12	60
2:7	63	22:14-15	36

Topical Index

Angels, their interest in salvation, 83-85
Apostles, the
    identity of, 82-83
    proclamation of, 82-83

Barclay, William, on various trials, 48-49
Barnhouse, Donald Grey, on the hungry Scotsman, 52-53
Bernard of Clairvaux, "Jesus Thou Joy of Loving Hearts," 68
Blessing. See God, blessing
Born again. See Regeneration

Charnock, Stephen, on the new birth, 31-32
Crackers-and-cheese Christians, 52-53

Deliverance. See Salvation

Faith
    persevering. See Perseverance of the saints
    proved, 47-53
    testing. See proved
Father, the. See God, fatherhood of
Fellowship, divine, 62-66

Glorification, 58-62
God
    adoring, 7-39, 63-66
    blessing, 16-17, 20-21
    compassion of. See mercy of
    fatherhood of, 17-19
    grace of. See Grace
    loving. See adoring
    mercy of, 25-27, 39
    praising. See adoring, blessing
Grace
    extent of, 74-76
    nature of, 73-74
Gurnall, William, on hope, 33

Happiness. See Joy
Heaven, inheriting, 29
Hell, inheriting, 29
Holy Spirit, the
    inspiration by. See Inspiration
    joy and, 46
    pledge of, 15
Honor
    divine. See Glorification
    human, 69
Hope
    basis of, 32-33, 39
    nature of, 32

Inheritance
    concept of, 9-16
    earthly, 35
    heavenly. See Salvation
    Israel's, 11, 14-15
Inspiration
    fact of, 80
    focus of, 81
    fulfillment of, 81-82
    process of, 80-81
Israel
    grace of God toward. See Grace, extent of
    inheritance of. See Israel

Jesus Christ
    deity of. See sonship of

93

loving, 63-66
sonship of, 17-19
"Jesus, I Am Resting," 67-68
"Jesus, Thou Joy of Loving
    Hearts," 68
Joy
    companions of, 43-44
    the Holy Spirit and, 46
    the psalms and, 56-57
    the resurrection and, 45
    salvation. *See* Salvation
    theme of, 42
    threats to, 42-43
    trials and, *See* Trials

Kistemaker, Simon J., on "ob-
    taining" in 1 Peter 1:9, 66

Leighton, Robert, on loving
    Christ, 65
Lenski, R. C. H.
    on Christ's redemptive name,
    19
    on persevering faith, 37

Mercy, God's. *See* God
Messiah, studying the. *See*
    Prophets, study of the
Money, treasure in heaven, 35

Nicodemus, Jesus' discussion
    with, 29-31
New birth, the. *See*
    Regeneration

Old Testament, prophets of the.
    See Prophets

Persecution, joy and, 42-43
Perseverance of the saints, 37.
    See also Salvation, securi-
    ty of
Pigott, Jean Sophia, "Jesus, I
    Am Resting," 67-68

Praise, receiving. *See*
    Glorification
Prophecy
    of the prophets. *See* Prophets
    of salvation. *See* Salvation
Prophets, study of the, 73-80
Psalms, joy and the. *See* Joy

Regeneration
    importance of, 31-33
    nature of, 28-32
    result of, 32-33
Reinecker, Fritz
    on "favor" in 1 Peter 1:7, 59
    on "greatly rejoice" in 1 Peter
    1:6, 44
    on "imperishable" in 1 Peter
    1:4, 33
    on "inheritance" in 1 Peter
    1:4, 10
    on "joy inexpressible" in
    1 Peter 1:8, 66
    on "protected" in 1 Peter 1:5,
    36-37
    on "reserved" in 1 Peter 1:4,
    35
    on "souls" in 1 Peter 1:9, 67
    on "will not fade away" in
    1 Peter 1:4, 35
Resurrection, the
    hope and, 32-33
    joy and, 45
Rogers, Cleon. *See* Reinecker,
    Fritz

Salvation
    affirmation of, 9-10
    angels and. *See* Angels
    anticipating, 16
    completion of. *See* security of
    deliverance of, 66-67
    description of, 10-15
    fellowship of, 63-66
    glorification. *See* Glorification

greatness of, 71-87
guarantee of. *See* proof of
honor of, 58-62
joy of, 41-69. *See* also preciousness of
looking forward to. *See* anticipating
means of, 28-33
motive of, 25-27
nature of, 33-35, 45
preciousness of, 79, 85-87. *See* also joy of
prophecy of, 73-87
proof of, 45-46
receiving. *See* glorification
remembering our, 7-16
security of, 13-14, 35-38, 42-47, 66-67
source of, 16-20
studying, 71-87
tenses of, 13-14
Scotsman, the hungry, 52-53
Scripture
inspiration of. *See* Inspiration
Old Testament. *See* Old Testament
studying, 71-87

Security, of salvation. *See* Salvation
Sin, its effect on joy, 42
Spurgeon, Charles H., on joy and trials, 58
Suffering. *See* Trials

Thankfulness. *See* God, blessing
Treasure. *See* Inheritance
Trials
duration of, 48
faith in the midst of, 47-52
joy in the midst of, 42-69
pain of, 48
purpose of, 47-52
responding to, 53-54
self-imposed, 53-54
types of, 48-49, 53-54
welcoming, 52
Trinity, designation of the, 17-19

Watson, Thomas, on God's mercy, 26
Wuest, Kenneth, on Ephesians 2:8, 13